I Am! I Can!

A Preschool Curriculum

Activities for the Classroom

I Am! I Can!

A Preschool Curriculum

Activities for the Classroom

New and Revised

Harriet Chmela
Grace L. Mitchell
Lois F. Dewsnap

Illustrations by Harriet Chmela and Ted Dewan

TelShare Publishing Company, Inc.
Chelsea, Mass.

Printed in the United States of America
Library of Congress Catalog Card Number: 91-67110
ISBN: 0-910287-10-4

Illustrations by Harriet Chmela and Ted Dewan

Second Printing, January 1999.

TABLE OF CONTENTS

ACKNOWLEDGEMENTS

The authors wish to express their gratitude to the many teachers who contributed their original ideas, creative efforts and practical suggestions to this work. To list them all would be an impossible task—rather let it be said that their generosity is symbolic of the spirit of sharing which is typical of our profession.

As we prepared to do this revision, we asked people who have been using the original book to give us their suggestions for changes and improvements. We are especially grateful to Edith Counter Duran, Kathy Knowler, Susan Pollack and Charlyne Taylor for giving so generously of their time in their responses.

We would be remiss if we did not give special thanks to Larry and Leah Rood, whose practical advice was only surpassed by their warm encouragement. Our gratitude also to Liz Webster, our typesetter, who accepted our endless changes and corrections with unfailing patience and cheerfulness.

And, of course, we are deeply appreciative of our families, especially to the new generation—Melyssa (10) and Alyson (12), who searched out the best recipe for making bubbles, and Holly (10) who worked with "Nana" Harriet all summer. Her sage child's-eye view of the activities was invaluable.

DEDICATED TO ALL WHO WONDER

To Albina Selevko and Galina Evstifeeva, their teaching colleagues and students at the Nekrasov School, Yaroslavyl, Russia—alive with renewed spirit as their curiosity and enthusiasm for knowledge nourishes the growing edges of a new nation,

and

To all of you who read this, and the children who will teach you how to wonder. Keep searching for answers, remembering that it is in the act of seeking that learning happens.

THINGS YOU NEED TO KNOW
IN USING THIS BOOK

1. This book is *sequential*, each sequence, or chapter, building on the ones before it. For example, the PEOPLE theme moves from the child to the family, to the extended family, to the community. If a child enters during the school year, go back to the activities missed in earlier sequences.

2. The book is also *thematic*. Each Sequence has several themes. One may be inspired by the time of year—for example, Halloween is a theme in October—while others may be quite different. The themes will give you many activities the children will enjoy, regardless of their developmental stage.

3. Each Sequence has an introductory page which gives you a sense of what is covered that month. If you read all twelve of them, you will have an overview of the whole book.

4. Each activity has an age code, with *suggested* ages. We know very well that a wide range of ability can be found at any chronological age. We also know many teachers will adapt an activity to fit the ages of the children in a certain class—so allow for flexibility as you look at the age codes.

5. Beginning on page 197, you will find a two part Index. Part One lists the activities under main headings, so if you wanted to do things with Bubbles, for example, all activities related to Bubbles would be listed together. Part Two is an alphabetical listing of all the activities. If you wanted to find a specific activity, such as Helicopter Twirls, you would look for it here.

6. The authors of this book are from New England, so you will find the book is oriented to that area. Adapt the themes and activities to that which is appropriate in *your* part of the world.

7. Volume One contains detailed information that relates closely to these activities. Example, this book suggests many field trips. Volume One gives you practical advice on planning, from a detailed permission slip to transportation arrangements, safety precautions, goals and followup.

8. An understanding of the "I AM! I CAN!" philosophy provides the foundation for all you do in the classroom. Turn the page for Dr. Mitchell's explanation of this.

THE I AM! I CAN! PHILOSOPHY

This diagram depicts a frame for the "I AM! I CAN!" philosophy. The four sides of the square represent the four areas of human growth and development.

A child grows in all four of the areas shown on the square, but growth will not be balanced or equal in all areas at all times. At times, physical growth is rapid, at others the child is bursting with ideas and creative energy. There come times when the need for the companionship of peers is uppermost, while emotional growth will reach highs and lows. A sudden spurt in one direction will often be followed by a plateau—a quiet time when the growing individual seems to be absorbing and assimilating what has been experienced.

The four corners of the square can be compared to the sharp edges of a personality. On the social side of "becoming" we rub against others, learn to compromise and adjust, and little by little those sharp corners are honed away. The square is moving in the direction of the circle.

The circle within the square, representing the "well-rounded" personality, is as mythical as the perfect human being. In a world abounding in variety and differences, there is a place for everyone. Each must seek the particular place in life which will allow the full use of individual skills, talents, and interests.

The "I AM!" comes through development of a healthy ego, through accepting oneself as a worthwhile human being—needed, wanted, liked, LOVED—and at all times, in all things—BEING ACCEPTED AS IS.

The arrows in the diagram indicate that when this is the case, the child can approach each new developmental task with confidence and meet with success. Each new success strengthens the "I CAN!" which in turn reinforces the "I AM!," and the beautiful circular motion thus established can go on *ad infinitum.*

The human personality in the developing process might be compared to the human figure in the growing process, bulging in one spot today, sticking out in another next week, or being completely lopsided for an extended period. The I AM! I CAN! philosophy does not seek to create perfect patterns of the square and circle, but uses the image symbolically to define a basic philosophy of education.

What happens to this very young, developing person who is constantly put down, denied inherent rights to physical and psychological protection, thwarted, discouraged, labeled by society as a misfit or a dropout? This continual assault on the "I AM!" will make it impossible for the child to become a competent, contributing member of society. The lack of decent self image will destroy the "I AM!" and will cancel out any hope of developing the "I CAN!"

Teachers have a responsibility to constantly evaluate *total* development, to be aware of the progress of each child in each area of growth at *all* times. They observe children with this pattern in mind, seeing them as individuals, not just members of a group.

There will always be children who are at one end or the other of a continuum, either bright, attractive children who make teaching a joy, or the ones who, because of their behavior or personality, are hard to love. In between these two extremes are the "deprived" children, neither "good" nor "bad" enough to be noticed. They go through life unnoticed, never receiving the extra attention which might develop their full potential. The true teacher sees and appreciates each and every child. Though each one deserves and should receive a full share of time and attention, it is neither possible nor necessary that they all receive *equal shares*, since needs vary, both within groups and within individuals. The child who is suddenly bursting with creative energy after a month of easy social growth needs to be stimulated and challenged. The teacher who has kept lap and arms ready for the shy and insecure child intuitively senses when to pull back and let go, or when to give a gentle nudge of encouragement.

A teacher will know which child can climb the ladder on the slide, which one is poorly coordinated, which one is trying to find a friend, cautiously working toward becoming a social being. It is important also to recognize biting, kicking and grabbing behavior as another form of social awakening. A teacher can "read" the frustration of a child through the language of behavior. As that child, guided by the teacher, accepts the fact that life is not always perfect, one of the sharp corners of the developmental square will be chipped away.

Every teacher thrills to see the glow of success on the face of a child, and strives to create opportunities for that success—EVERY DAY!

The activities in this book can be used to stimulate healthy growth in all areas of development, enabling each child to say, "I AM! I CAN!"

How does the "I AM! I CAN!" philosophy apply to curriculum?

A curriculum which is not based on a sound philosophy is like the house built on sand. A teacher of young children needs to "frame in" a set of beliefs and values in order to determine what is best for children. It isn't enough to feel it—it must be put into words and then into action. Once the philosophy is stated, it must be so much a part of the teacher that it will automatically become a yardstick against which to measure a program. This can be done by asking oneself—

Will this activity contribute to development on at least one side of the square by:

- Fostering physical growth?
- Improving coordination?
- Allowing for social interaction?
- Stimulating the thought process?
- Adding to knowledge?
- Providing the opportunity for choices?
- Sharpening reasoning skills?

When teachers carry a visual image of the square and circle, with that little child in the center, will they see the exuberant, enthusiastic robust four year old with an inquiring mind? Will they envision the shy trusting little one who clings to an outstretched hand? Will they be alert to that "average" child who also needs their attention?

When each child is seen as a unique individual, the teacher will instinctively know what is needed for the development of a healthy personality; will plan not one program "for my group" but individualized programs for each child.

The philosophy is the "WHY" of program. Part of the "HOW" lies in knowing how to create an environment in which individual growth is possible. Well designed learning centers open up a range of opportunities to arouse the interest and test the skills of each child.

A more detailed description of the way to create an environment in which the "WHAT" and "HOW" can flourish will be found in Volume One, *Keys to Quality Child Care*.

The "I AM! I CAN!" philosophy is the foundation on which the curriculum is based. Volume One gives you the bricks and mortar for that foundation.

SEQUENCE ONE

SEPTEMBER

SEPTEMBER THEMES

SEPTEMBER

Cozy Laps and Stars in Apples

The major goal of this first sequence is to strengthen the *"I Am"* of each child. A young child entering child care leaves the familiar and *secure feeling* of home. <u>Every</u> staff member—teachers, aides, cook, director—knows and *greets* each child by *name*. Every child is assured, "They know my name and where I live. Someone can help me call Mummy or Daddy if I need them."

Songs, stories, *familiar nursery rhymes* and games using names reassure and reinforce each child's self-image. Activities based on familiar concepts—*round* and *red; up* and *down; high* and *low*—strengthen the *"I Can"* of the children. As teachers and children sing *"Good Morning"* songs, or *"The More We Are Together,"* they make new *friends* and learn their names.

Children traveling to and from child care learn to use *seat belts* or *crosswalks* and *traffic signals* for *safety*. *Police* and *crossing guards* help to teach *"Red* means stop and *green* means go."

Careful and patient teaching of simple *rules and routines* such as *hand washing* and *putting things away*; making a *special place* (cubbies) for "my things"; keeping "Teddy" nearby for a few days for <u>security</u>, will help children *adjust* to and be comfortable in their new environment.

Give lonesome little helpers the responsibility for tucking a *sock doll* into its *cradle* when they need a special friend to cuddle.

"I made *cinnamon toast* all by myself! We went to an *orchard* and picked some apples. Mrs. Brook told us a story about an apple. The apple had a *star inside*."

Many of the sequences teach children something about the importance and usefulness of *trees*. We begin in September with apple trees and their juicy, delicious fruit. We also teach how to *conserve and recycle paper*, one of the most common uses of trees.

Children are generally curious, not repelled by "icky" bugs as adults sometimes are. Respect and encourage "bug watching" using nature books as guides. Lady bugs are "user friendly."

When children draw or paste pictures into folders and the teacher adds words or sentences dictated by the child, the children have become authors of their first *books*.

It is very difficult sometimes to say *"goodbye." Separation* from family and familiar places takes *practice*. Children gain confidence as they play *"Hello and Goodbye" games*. They can even learn some new words for these *greetings*. Children who live in faraway places say *"Bon jour," "Buon giorno"* or *"Buenas dias"* to greet their parents (but their hugs and kisses feel the same).

No matter how mummy and daddy say "goodbye," a child feels sad and lonesome when they go away. But, a *cozy lap always ready* for a cuddle—for a little while—(JUST FOR FUN) helps a child feel safe and secure once again, then "I Can do anything."

SEQUENCE ONE

PEOPLE

|5|
|↑|
|2|

Rolling A Name

Sit in a circle. Roll a ball to (Robert). Say: "I am rolling the ball to (Robert)." "I am rolling the ball to (Holly)."

When children are familiar with the game and each other, they can take turns rolling the ball and calling names.

|5|
|↑|
|3|

Guess Who?

"I am thinking of a girl wearing a red shirt. Who is it?" A child who responds chooses a different child to describe.

At first, adults may need to take three or four turns. When children repeat previous descriptions, ask: "What other colors?" or "Choose another person."

|5|
|↑|
|3|

Rhyming Names

Use child's name in a rhyme. "You are Matt, you wear a hat." "You are Paul, you're very tall." "June, June, tap your spoon." "Mary, Mary, jump to Larry."

For hard-to-rhyme names, make up nonsense words.

|5|
|↑|
|2|

Match-A-Name

Place four to six snapshots of children on individual cards. Print names of children on matching cards.

Children match names with own pictures, later matching names of other children to their pictures. Children could wear name labels to aid in matching name cards.

TODDLERS, TOO! Point to toddler's picture, saying the name. Holding toddler's hand, touch the picture, asking "Who is this?"

|5|
|↑|
|3|

Name Tree

- "Plant" a twiggy branch in a tub of plaster. Paint/color cardboard apples. Attach ties and add names. Hang apples on tree.

  Variation: Make a large cardboard tree. Attach Velcro patches to limbs and apples. Put cards in a basket.

- Attendance: Child locates his/her apple in basket and hangs it on the tree.

- Game: Each child chooses an apple. Teacher reads name. Child locates owner, who hangs it on the tree.

- Counting: All count the apples on the tree to see how many children are present.

- Change apples for other symbols during year: leaves, mittens, colored eggs, etc.

| 5 ↑ 2 | ### Self Portraits |

For this you will need paper long enough for child's full body length. Rolls of paper such as used to cover tables are best.

a. Child lies down on paper, arms slightly away from the sides. Trace around child.

b. Child looks carefully at reflection in a full length mirror, then colors in own portrait with crayons.

c. Cut across top and bottom of paper; put name and date on paper; display for a while.

d. Put away, to be used later in the year. (See April—PEOPLE—*Self-Image—A New Look*)

EXPANDING OUR WORLD

| 4 ↑ 2 | ### Saying Goodbye |

Practice saying "Goodbye," as children take turns leaving the room for a few moments.

When an adult leaves the room, say, "Goodbye, Miss Julie."

Explain, "Miss Julie is going to the office, she will be right back." When she returns, say, "She came back."

| 4 ↑ 2 | ### Goodbye Kit |

Ask parents to assemble, with child's help, a collection of six to eight familiar items—family snapshot, favorite small toy or book, perhaps a taped message by a parent.

Keep the "Goodbye Kit" in the child's cubby, for emergency use only.

When the child no longer needs the kit, send it home. Say, "You're bigger, you don't need those toys any more."

| 5 ↑ 3 | ### Cook |

Take four to six children to meet the cook.

- Practice Good Morning greetings, repeating names.

- Ask: "What are you cooking?"

- Look for and name tools used for various jobs.

- Tell and dramatize stories after visit.

- Combine this activity with *Saying Goodbye*. Send one child to visit the cook and return.

- This procedure may be followed by visits to others, such as secretary, maintenance person, etc.

| 5 ↑ 3 | ### Police Officer/Station |

- Visit a nearby police station or invite an officer to visit, in a cruiser, to demonstrate equipment, talk about the various items worn with the uniform and describe the everyday duties of police officers.

- Walk to a crosswalk while safety officers are on duty. Practice crossing skills.

- Invite a crossing guard to come to the center between school crossing times for mid-morning snack. Play *Crosswalk Playmates* with a real officer.

Apple Orchard/Fruit Stand

up
↑
3

Visit places where apples are grown, processed or sold.

- Pick some if possible. Walk around under the trees, hug a tree.
- Count variety of apples sold.
- Look for products made with apples.
- Notice things pickers use: ladders, long poles, baskets.
- Compare colors, shapes, and markings on apples.
- What other jobs are people doing? (packing, weighing, selling)

SKILLS FOR DAILY LIVING

Space of My Own (Names, Adjustment)

up
↑
2

Every child needs a space for personal belongings. The following activities will help children understand how to identify this space.

- Print child's name on a card and tack it to or above the space.
- Place child's snapshot beside the name.
- Ask the child to find a picture of an animal, bird, flower, truck, etc. to put there.

Hand Washing

5
↑
2

Carefully, slowly, and *daily* demonstrate this routine. Hand washing is not something done before or after an activity—it *is* an activity. Allow time to:

a. Wet hands under warm water. Lather with soap.

b. Rub lather on palms, backs of hands and wrists. Suds between fingers. Brush under nails.

c. Rinse and dry. Shake off excess water, then use *one* towel to dry hands. (Paper conservation)

Fours and fives might sing, "This is the way I wash (scrub, dry) my hands." Time spent in singing the jingle helps slow the process for a thorough washing.

Seat Belt Rhymes

up
↑
2

When I'm riding in a car,
Riding near or riding far,
I snap the seat belt for I know,
I'll be safe at fast or slow.

Huckle, chuckle, buckle up!
Click it, clack it, push it shut.
Pull it out, then push it in,
Wear a belt and wear your grin!

| 5 ↑ 3 | *Crosswalk Playmates (Left/Right)*

Stop, look and listen, Before you cross the street.

First use your eyes and ears, Then use your feet.

Make a crosswalk with lines or masking tape on the floor, or paint yellow lines on a strip of roofing paper or a rubber runner.

Children take turns crossing the "street." Remind, "Look both ways," or "Look right, look left, look right again."

CONCEPTS

| 5 ,↑ 3 | *Up/Down—High/Low*
- Pour water/sand into containers to different levels, high, low.
- Place a plank on a slight incline and walk or crawl up/down.
- Suspend balloons high/low and bat them with paper tubes.

CAUTION: Remove burst balloons immediately. TODDLERS may choke on pieces of rubber.

| 5 ↑ 3 | *Red Trail (Language)*

Make a "Red Trail" using chalk, paper, ribbon, red footprints. Place red objects along the trail. Children follow the trail and bring back the objects, or come back and tell you what they saw.

| 5 ↑ 3 | *Red Reflections*

Tape red cellophane or tissue to a sunny window. "Catch" reflections on white paper.

| up ↑ 4 | *Mixing Red*

Use eyedroppers to drop food color into small containers of water. Try to create shades of light to dark tones.

| up ↑ 3 | *Circles/Rounds*

Children bring round objects—circles, globes, spheres—to a round table, hoop, rug, or marked circle.
- Mark or place a circular patch in the center. Roll a ball into the circle.
- Bounce real (or imaginary) balls to each other, call names. ("I'm bouncing the ball to Jerry. Jerry, bounce it to Fred.")
- Take turns tossing balls into a large trash can. SCHOOL AGE keep score.

SCIENCE

Discovery Table

Encourage interests and hobbies of children by providing a display space. Children help to establish simple rules, such as:

1. Label items. Identify with child's name.

2. How long displays remain. (Keep them fresh!)

3. Number of children at the display at one time.

(This is a better way of sharing than the traditional "Show and Tell.")

Apples (Round, Red, Math)

up ↑ 2

A crisp apple eaten after a meal helps to clean the teeth.

Apples, besides their nutritional values, can be used in many activities, such as:

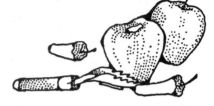

- Taste them: raw, cooked, dried. (TEXTURE)
- Cut in halves, quarters. (MATH)
- Make juice into popsicles, and jello. (MEASURING)
- Bake whole, serve with yogurt. (TASTING)
- Slice into rings to reveal the star. (See below)
- TODDLERS, TOO! Shake-in-a-Jar: apple sauce, milk, dash of vanilla.

Little Red House

up ↑ 3

One bright fall morning, a little boy asked his mother, as I know you have asked *your* mother many times, "What can I do, Mommy?"

His mother, who knew lots of happy things for boys to do, smiled and said, "I think this is just the sort of morning to spend looking for the little red house."

"What little red house?" asked the little boy.

"Oh," replied his mother, "the little red house with no doors and no windows and a star inside."

"No doors and no windows and a star inside?" asked the little boy. "What kind of a house is that?"

"A very special house," answered his mother.

"How can I find that little red house?" asked the little boy.

"I think Mr. Wind could help you. Why don't you go out in the backyard and ask him?"

So the little boy put on the warm, blue sweater his mother had knit for him and went out into the backyard. He stood under the big old apple tree and called, "Mr. Wind, Mr. Wind, please help me find the little red house with no doors and no windows and a star inside."

At that, Mr. Wind, high in the top of the apple tree, chuckled. When he chuckled, the leaves whispered together and the branches swayed, and down fell a beautiful big red apple, right at the little boy's feet.

He picked the apple up and looked at it carefully and then he began to chuckle, too. "Thank you, Mr. Wind," he called as he ran back into the house.

"Mother, mother," he called, "I think I have it!" He put the big apple on his mother's kitchen table. "It's red and has no doors and no windows," he said, "but is it a house and does it have a star inside?"

"Yes," said his mother, "it is a house, and a very special house it is, too. It is the home for tiny apple seeds—seeds that can someday grow into strong new apple trees with lots and lots of beautiful little red houses on them."

Then his mother took the apple and washed it. She rubbed it with a soft cloth until it shone. She took a sharp knife and cut across the apple. There, to the little boy's surprise and delight, were the tiny seeds, nestled safely in a beautiful star.

Applesauce from Great Gram's Kitchen

up ↑ 2

3 lbs. apples	1/4 to 1/2 c. sugar, depending on tartness of apples
1/2 cup water	1/4 cup cinnamon "Red Hots" (candy)

a. Wash, quarter and core apples.

b. Heat apples and water to boiling. Turn down heat and simmer until apples are soft.

c. Press pulp through a colander or food mill into another pan.

d. Add sugar and "Red Hots," cook on low heat, stirring constantly, until candies melt.

Note: You may use 1/2 tsp. cinnamon, but the candies give a lovely pink color as well as flavor.

Grapes to Raisins (Before/After)

up ↑ 4

"What are they? How do they grow?"

Weigh, then hang, bunches of red and green grapes in a sunny window. Note the daily changes in size, color and texture (approximately two weeks.) Some will form molds, natural to the process.

- When dried and shriveled, remove and count.
- Compare appearance, taste, and weight, before and after.
- Compare with commercial raisins.

Cinnamon Toast

up ↑ 2

Mix sugar and cinnamon in shakers to sprinkle onto buttered toast. Top with banana slices or apple sauce for added nutrition. Children can slice bananas with plastic knives.

TODDLERS, TOO!

Beetles

up ↑ 3

Beetles are "user friendly" creatures for children to catch and observe. Beetles eat grubs, caterpillars, meal worms. Rotten wood containing soft insects and eggs will also provide food. Look in nature guides to identify and maintain your particular beetle.

- A beetle trap can be made by burying an empty can in the ground, rim even with the surface. Put some syrup or wet sugar in the can.
- Homes for observing and caring for beetles can be made in terrariums. Cover top with screening, do not close lids. Put two to three inches of soil in bottom. Keep moist, not wet. Provide drinking water in a *shallow* dish. (See July—SCIENCE—*Insect Foods*)

September

Pets

up ↑ 3

Check with local and state health regulations as to what animals are allowed in centers and how much children can be involved in the care of animals, i.e. handling and feeding.

- Introduce pets to two or three children at a time.

- Use pictures of household pets to make books about "My Pet." Ask: "What's your pet's name? What does it eat? Where does it sleep? What color is it?"

- Talk about the ways our pets are like or different from us. (Food, shelter, families, work, play.)

Apple Trees

up ↑ 4

Display photographs of apple trees in various seasons. Invite a nurseryman or fruit grower to visit and/or provide materials.

Cut open an apple to show seeds and protective hull. Carve away all of apple to show the entire seed pod. Experiment with planting the seeds.

Rooting

up ↑ 3

Begonias (non-tuberous) can be easily rooted by putting cuttings in water. Cut 2-3 inch pieces from a large plant. Remove lower leaves. Submerge stem in a small container of water, such as a clear spice bottle, so children can watch for the tiny root hairs as they form.

Keep the water level over the rooting stem. When roots are 1" to 2" long, transplant cuttings into small pots (paper cups) full of soil.

Replant rooted seedlings into larger pots and place in a sunny window. Plants grown in a window will grow towards the light. Experiment by turning some plants and leaving others to bend in one direction.

Paper Conservation and Recycling

up ↑ 4

Trees are a major source of paper. It takes many years to grow one tree. Stress the importance of conserving, re-using and recycling paper products. Look for "Recycled" logo on products.

- Children make a display of the paper products they can find in the center. Put pictures of trees or green triangles on products which use paper, as a reminder.

- Involve children in recycling jobs. Provide sorting bins for glass, paper, plastic and metal. Show how papers can be folded and compacted to save space in containers.

- Sometimes trash is dumped at landfills. Landfills fill up and more dumps are needed. Show one way to save space. Using two equal piles of folded newspaper, set one pile in carton, and mark a line on carton at top of pile. Remove pile of papers. Ask children to wrinkle second pile, sheet by sheet, and toss into the same carton. They will see the difference. SCHOOL AGE

Trash/Decomposition

up ↑ 5

Demonstrate how some trash decomposes in a matter of months, while other trash will remain the same for many years.

Bury some paper, glass, plastic and metal trash in several test batches, using one item from each category in each batch. Mark the spots with the date of burial and a second date when you plan to dig up each one at (2, 6, 10, 12 month) intervals.

At the end, set up an exhibit showing the results of each test. SCHOOL AGE

5 ↑ 3 | *Spoons (Seriation, Sets)*
Collect a variety of spoons, from tiny to a large cooking spoon. Include metal, wood, plastic.

- Arrange spoons from small to large.

- Put in sets: metal, wood, plastic.

- Set up a pattern of 3 to 4 spoons, ask children to copy.

- Mime the motions which show the use of a particular spoon— sipping, stirring, beating. Child chooses an appropriate spoon for the task.

up ↑ 5 | *Change-A-Shape (Problem Solving)*
Give child a sheet of paper; ask "How can you use all of this paper to make a different shape?"

MUSIC—MOVEMENT

5 ↑ 3 | *Good Morning, Little Yellow Bird (Names, Colors)*
Sing to each child, using color of garments and first and last name.
Teacher or Group:

> *"Good morning little (color) bird, (color) bird, (color) bird,*

> *"Good morning little (color) bird, who are you?"*

Child:

> *"My name is (Susan Applebee, Applebee, Applebee)*

> *"My name is (Susan Applebee), I'll tell you true."*

5 ↑ 3 | *Oh, the More We Are Together (Names)*

> *"Oh, the more we are together, together, together,*

> *"Oh, the more we are together, the happier we'll be,*

> *"For, it's Johnny and Kathy, and Sarah and Frannie,*

> *"Oh, the more we are together, the happier we'll be."*

up ↑ 2 | *Hands*
- Cut and mount on cards, pictures of hands and arms in various positions. Teacher holds up pictures for others to copy in exercises. Use pictures to reinforce Left/Right, Up/Down concepts.

- Show hands holding objects. Ask children to find the same object and hold the same way.

- Older children might learn some of the letters of the ISL or ASL (International or American Sign Language) (see unabridged dictionary).

TODDLERS mimic teacher's motions—"folded hands," "pointing fingers," "outstretched hands," "fists," "palms up/down."

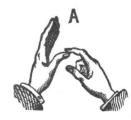

September

up ↑ 3
Finger Exercises (Spatial Concepts)

Stretch fingers. Bend them, make fists, squeeze tight, make little circles. Tap nails, walk fingers on the floor, up and down the arms. Fold fingers together and stretch arms way out, move from side to side. Place folded hands in lap. Try also with music.

5 ↑ 2
Five Red Apples (Finger Play)

Five red apples, hanging on a tree

The juiciest apples you ever did see

The wind came past with an angry frown

(Hold up hand, palm outward, fingers extended.)

One little apple came tumbling down.

(Tuck in one finger.)

(Four red apples, etc.)

(Tuck in a finger each time an apple falls.)

5 ↑ 3
Rig-A-Jig-Jig (Names)

Form a circle, choose "It". "It" walks around *inside*. Sing:

"As (name/I) was walking (skipping, hopping, crawling, etc.) down the street,

"Down the street, down the street,

"A little friend I chanced to meet

"Heigh-ho, heigh-ho, heigh-ho."

"It" stops before a child, says: "What is your name?" (loud, clear)

Answer in *complete sentence*: "My name is (Jamal)."

Two take hands and skip (hop, etc.) around *outside* of circle. All sing:

"Rig-a-jig-jig and away we go, away we go, away we go.

"Rig-a-jig-jig and away we go, heigh-ho, heigh-ho, heigh-ho."

As couple skip around, group claps (sways, swings, etc.) so all are involved in the motions.

First child ("It") returns to place and second child repeats the cycle.

4 ↑ 2
Jack-in-the-Box

Children scrunch down. Teacher says, in a mysterious voice: "Down in the box there lives a little man. He waits and he waits as quiet as he can. Until the lid goes POP!"

Vary the tempo, sometimes quick, then s-l-o-w, then quick. Sometimes very, very slow, building the suspense. Whisper. Grow louder, soft again. At the final word, all POP UP!

TODDLERS, TOO!

up ↑ 4
Hoops (Creative Movement)

Lay a hoop on the floor. Sit/stand around it. Ask:

"Who can go around the hoop?"

"Who can think of a different way?" (Hop, skip, roll, jump in and out, etc.)

Can you go *through* the hoop?

"What can two (3, 4, etc.) people do with the hoop?"

5 ↑ 3 **Traffic Light Chant (Movement, Left/Right)**

I love to skip, skip, skip.

I love to hop, hop, hop.

But when I see a red light

I stop, stop, stop.

I look to the left.

I look to the right.

And then I push the button

On the traffic light.

When the light says "Walk,",

Then I know

That it's surely safe to go.

5 ↑ 3 **One, Two, Buckle My Shoe (Counting)**

Use the traditional counting rhymes and also extend ideas in variations:

"One, two, who are you?"

"Three, four, tap the floor."

"Five, six, where is Dick?"

up ↑ 4 **Body-Mind Stretcher (Spatial Concepts)**

Move across the room as if crawling through a large pipe, crossing stepping stones, gliding on ice, etc.

LANGUAGE—DRAMA

5 ↑ 2 **Nursery Rhymes**

Children learn and act out familiar nursery rhymes.

"Little Miss Muffet"

"Jack and Jill"

"Humpty Dumpty" and others.

up ↑ 4 **My Own Book (Names, Words)**

Provide blank books for beginning writers to copy letters, numerals, names, and words that *they* have *learned*. Write the child's name on the cover as it should be written. Child might also wish to paste/draw in pictures which illustrate words learned.

Note: Leave school oriented activities, such as this, open to children's choice.

up ↑ 4 **Theme Books (Various Concepts, Categories)**

Children, in groups or alone, paste/draw pictures into Theme Books—"Red," "Dogs," "Round," "Loud," "Cold," "Flowers," "My Family," "I Can!"

up ↑ 4 **My Favorite Things**

Play and/or sing the song (from "The Sound of Music"). Make a list of favorite things of the group. Cut or draw pictures and paste on a mural or in book(s).

5 ↑ 3 **Complete Sentence (Language Skills)**

Encourage children to respond with complete sentences.

"My name is (_____)." (instead of a one-word response)

September

5 ↑ 3
Stories on Tape
Read and tell stories on tape. Play back, encourage responses during (planned) pauses. Use different voices. Add sound effects and music.

5 ↑ 3
Voice
Ask each child to say a name (or words) into a tape machine. Play back.
Say, "Raise your hand when you hear your voice."

up ↑ 4
Good Morning and Good Night (Multi-Cultural)
Teach how children in other countries say these familiar phrases.

Good morning	Good night	Language
Bon jour	Bon nûit	French
Buenas dias	Buenas noces	Spanish
Buon giorno	Buona notte	Italian

Ask children from other backgrounds (German, Chinese, Russian, etc.) to teach phrases in their language.

SCHOOL AGE children can extend this by finding the countries on a map of the world.

CREATIVE PROJECTS

up ↑ 4
Apples To Make (Recipe)
Form "apples" from sculpture material. Insert real twigs with leaves for stems. Dry and paint.
PAPIER MÂCHÉ

> Tear newsprint, paper towels and other absorbent papers into small pieces. Soak for two or three days. Add wheat (wallpaper) paste to produce a thick, mushy consistency. Add one teaspoon boric acid to prevent mildew and some drops of wintergreen as a preservative.

PLAY DOUGH

> 2 cups flour—1 cup salt—food coloring as desired
>
> Mix in *about* one cup of water to a pliable consistency.

up ↑ 5
Stand-Up Apple Tree
Make a 3-D tree from cardboard. Children then paste red circles for apples on the tree.

Make two tree shapes. Cut 1/4" slits in top of A, bottom of B. Slip two shapes together and open to right angles to stand up.

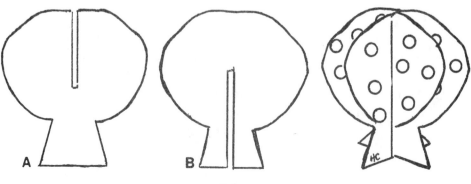

Cradle and Sock Doll

up ↑ 4

Stuff sock with cloth scraps. Tie off toe to create head. Mark on eyes. Wrap doll in blanket.

Cut away side section of an oatmeal box to create a cradle.

Casts

up ↑ 5

Pack wet sand into shallow (5" to 8" deep) carton lined with plastic. Pat to smooth surface. Press objects into sand to create circular impressions at various depths (small bottles, yogurt cups, dowels).

Pour a layer of plaster of paris into impressions and up to a 2"-3"depth over entire surface.

When plaster has set, lift off to reveal raised circular shapes.

WARNING! DO NOT wash plaster off hands and implements at the sink. Plaster will harden and clog drain. Rinse in separate container and empty outside.

Milk Carton Traffic Light

up ↑ 4

Cut three holes in one side of a milk carton. Cover each hole with green, red, or yellow tissue paper.

Cut a wide slit in opposite (back) of carton. Shine a flashlight through the colored panels for "Stop," "Go" traffic games.

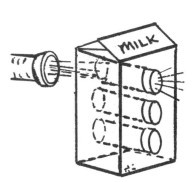

JUST FOR FUN

Teddy Bear Day (Adjustment)

up ↑ 3

Invite everyone to bring a favorite cuddly to share in various activities below.

Teddies are: held high/low, left/right—served pretend foods—traced around—introduced in name games—helped across the "street"—sorted by size, color, matched to owner—tucked in for naps.

Use this activity *after* children have settled into routines, to reinforce concepts.

TODDLERS, 2's should play these games with housekeeping corner toys as they may be unwilling to share cuddlies from home.

Bowling Games

up ↑ 4

Make pins from milk cartons, plastic bottles or cardboard tubes with one end sealed. Add weight with pebbles or sand. Seal top.

Mark pins with colors, numerals, dots (1, 2, 3, etc.).

Mark matching places to set pins on "alley" floor.

Discuss and post rules (age appropriate).

> "Bowl 3 balls each turn."
>
> "Stand behind the red line."
>
> "Take turns setting up pins."

September

up ↑ 3

Shoe Talk (Sets, Motions)

Gather many kinds of shoes, boots, sneakers, slippers, in pairs.

Place in a box. Sit around the shoes.

One child chooses a shoe. Another finds the match. Or place a shoe behind each child. "It" chooses a shoe from box, walks around outside circle of children to find the match.

up ↑ 4

Block Towers

- Children sit in a circle. Blocks are piled in the center. Each takes a turn placing one block on a tower. When tower falls, clap! Start another.

- Older children (5's and up) each have 10 to 20 blocks. At a signal, all race to build towers.

- Divide into relay teams to build up towers. Blocks are on one end of room. One child from each team runs (hops, skips, crawls, etc.), places a block, returns (same motion). Second player goes to place block.

- Use cartons and boxes of various shapes and sizes instead of blocks.

CAUTION: Tumbling wooden blocks can injure babies/toddlers.

up ↑ 3

Bubbles (Recipe, Spatial Concepts)

Mix: 1/2 cup liquid dish detergent (Joy and Dawn work best) with 6 to 8 cups of water. For bigger, longer-lasting bubbles, add 1/4 cup Karo Syrup.

Song: to tune of "Did you ever see a lassie?"

Did you ever see a bubble, a bubble, a bubble,

Did you ever see a bubble, float high in the sky?

    Blow (drift, float) this way, blow that way,

    Come your way, come my way,

Did you see that pretty bubble go "Pop!" in my hair?

SEQUENCE TWO

OCTOBER

OCTOBER THEMES

Cotton Ball

Elastic

Kleenex

Stick

FINGER PUPPET GHOSTS

OCTOBER

Being Pumpkins and Discovering Skeletons

Children who have good feelings about themselves, their capabilities and who are comfortable and secure in their environment <u>can</u>: follow routines, create, and look beyond their familiar surroundings. Activities in this second sequence are designed to encourage children to **explore** and **discover**.

Every **family** does not have a father and a mother. Family profiles include many different life styles; economic and social groups; ethnic and cultural backgrounds. Gender, size, marital status—many factors define "family."

Families work and play together and apart. They love and share problems. Sometimes families disagree and separate, then reform. Children have step-parents, half-brothers/sisters, extra grandparents. All these factors affect a child's "I Am," and "I Can." Exploring, defining and claiming "My Family" aids the healthy emotional development of a young child.

Fire prevention and **drills** and **learning how to use a telephone** are the safety routines we can teach children during **fire safety month**.

It's October! **Pumpkins** are ripe on their vines and we will need to make **triangles**—the eyes and noses which turn **orange** pumpkins into **Jack O'Lanterns**.

Some traditional **Halloween** themes may frighten very young children. **"Dark," "skeletons," "ghosts,"** and **"monsters"** need to be discussed and acted out in an unthreatening manner. **Masks** and **costumes** help children pretend during dramatic play where they can be safe and comfortable. Masks do not have to be **scary**. Skeletons are not scary. They are the frameworks which support our bodies just as house frames serve a similar purpose.

We can teach children about the good nutrition in **yellow and orange vegetables** in contrast to the empty calories in candy and the sugary "treats" of Halloween.

Cats. Cat-ness is a rich theme. Through songs, stories, motions, dramatic play and creative projects children can learn much from these furry creatures—models of good living as children observe that cats **wash themselves** and **take naps** every day.

Monarch butterfly **cocoons** form on **milkweed** pods. Children can collect and hatch these lovely butterflies and launch them on their flights of **migration**.

Autumn and **harvests** are rich New England adventures. What seasonal changes are happening where you live?

Exploring, discovering—whether it is Columbus finding a new world or a four-year old discovering three kinds of autumn leaves and two ways to eat pumpkins—discovery is exciting— JUST FOR FUN—have a Pumpkin Toss!

SEQUENCE TWO

PEOPLE

up
↑
4

My Family (Self Image)
- Make up family "portraits" using photographs, paper dolls, magazine pictures or children's drawings. Construct from cloth, wallpaper and trims.
- Name and count family members.
- Use all the pictures to make a collage.

up
↑
4

Family Album (Language Development)
Use some of the pictures created in the first activity to make up an album. Add stories, comments and descriptions dictated by the children.

up
↑
2

Firefighters
Invite a firefighter to come in uniform. Display the big boots and hat. Hold the hat under running water to show how it helps keep the firefighter dry.

EXPANDING OUR WORLD

up
↑
5

Fire Station/Truck
Older children may enjoy a trip to the station. Sudden alarms and loud engines speeding off on an emergency may frighten younger children.

Sometimes fire equipment comes to a center for routine inspection. You may be able to arrange such a visit for younger children to see the fire trucks.

up
↑
3

Pumpkin Farm/Market
Children prepare in advance of their trip by deciding:
- How many and how big pumpkins should be. What other things they will see or buy at the farm—corn stalks, squash, hay for scarecrows, Indian corn, etc.
- Can they see the vines and bring some back? Can they pick their own pumpkins?
- If you take the children to the same place you went to for apples, what was different this time?

5
↑
3

My Trip to Child Care
The child's day in child care begins and ends with a ride. Children can tell stories and make books about these experiences. Help them with questions which suggest things to watch for such as:
- Who drives the car? Who is riding in the car? Does a playmate share the ride?
- Do you come by bus, subway or in a van? How else?
- What do you see? Tall buildings? Farms? Animals? Schools? Bridges?
- Do you see many people driving or walking along the route? Do some ride bicycles?
- What do you hear? Trains? Sirens? Bells? Horns? Machines? Birds? Tractors?

SKILLS FOR DAILY LIVING

| 5 |
| ↑ |
| 3 |

Washing Tables (Hygiene, Math, Routines)

Use small wash basins and sponges. Follow step-by-step procedures to wash tables. Say the steps aloud as you do it.

STEPS FOR WASHING TABLES

Pour warm water into pan up to second knuckle of your longest finger ("Tall Man"). This instruction helps to prevent over-filling the basin.

Put sponge(s) in basin.

Carry basin to table.

Squeeze excess water from sponge(s).

Wipe/wash each section.

Rinse and squeeze sponge(s). Rewipe area. Repeat as needed.

Carry basin and sponge(s) to sink. Rinse basin and sponge(s).

Wipe sink area. Rinse and squeeze sponge(s), and store.

| up |
| ↑ |
| 5 |

Fire Safety Procedures/Rules

Regularly take children on a tour of the center. Point to **exit** signs. In addition to **exit** signs posted high over doors/windows, post **exit** signs at child-high levels.

Demonstrate the **alarm** sound. Explain, "It makes a loud noise but it helps us escape to safety. It also calls the fire truck so we only use it when we want them to come."

Meet with the children to discuss, write down, and post **safety rules**, for example:

1. NO RUNNING/TALKING
2. DO NOT GO FOR COATS/BELONGINGS
3. WALK/CRAWL TO EXIT
4. GATHER OUTSIDE FOR A COUNT

After fire drills, look at the rules with the children. Were any rules broken?

| up |
| ↑ |
| 5 |

My Telephone Number (Safety, Adjustment, Language)

- Practice saying and dialing the number until children can repeat/dial accurately. An excellent activity with a child who needs reassurance or comfort. Say: "Speak clearly, say 'Hi, Mom, I'm practicing using a phone.'"

- Leave messages on answering machines. Ask parents to play back for child at home. Can they understand their own message?

- Use cards to match dial and touchtone phones to develop dialing skills.

  "Point to '0.' Point to the numbers in your phone number."

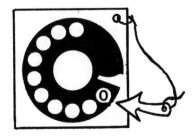
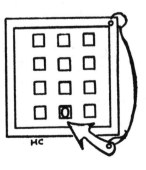

CONCEPTS

Morning/Noon/Night (Temporal)
`up ↑ 4`
- Ask: "When do you eat breakfast?" "See stars?" "Have naps?" "Go to bed?"
- Introduce a clock and clock pictures showing various times.
- Look for pictures of day/night activities. Arrange the pictures according to the times of the activities shown.

Over, Under, In and Out
`5 ↑ 2`
Give each child a small pumpkin (orange tennis ball) *or* scrunch orange paper into pumpkins. Give a box or plastic container big enough to hold the pumpkin. Sit in a circle.

"Put the pumpkin..." On top—inside—behind—under. Roll it into the box. TODDLERS, TOO!

Orange Surprise (Color)
`5 ↑ 3`
a. Mark a table top off into four sections with tape.
b. Put globs of finger paint, two red, two yellow, in opposite corners.
c. Fingerpaint! What happens to the colors as they blend?

Red Plus Yellow
`5 ↑ 3`
- Tempera: Use small plastic/paper cups or egg cartons. Give each child two portions of paint, red and yellow. Ask them to mix orange.
- Play dough: Use food colors to make orange play dough. Follow activity above. Can the children choose the correct combination of dyes?
- Crêpe paper: Dip strips of red and yellow crêpe paper into water and lay out in designs on white sheets (paper or cloth). What happens as the two colors overlap each other?

Scratch/Erase Orange
`up ↑ 4`
a. Color a heavy layer of red wax crayon over a layer of yellow wax crayon.
b. Scratch a design into the two layers. Hold paper up to the light so colors blend into orange.
c. Use an eraser to erase-blend two colors into smooth orange blend.

Orange Light
`up ↑ 2`
Hold red and yellow cellophane sheets up to window to blend orange.

Triangles (Shapes)
`up ↑ 4`
- Fold a square paper diagonally to create triangles.
- Draw/tape lines corner-to-corner on square and rectangular shapes (door panels, window panes, rugs, table tops, floor tiles, etc.).
- Cut triangle shapes from tiny to large. Hold shapes against pictures to match triangular objects (sailboats, bridge supports, rooftops, swing sets, road signs, steeples).
- Stress spatial descriptions as you develop ideas ("over/under," "beside," "long/short").

SCIENCE

Pumpkin Seeds, Baked

5
↑
3

a.   Pull seeds from pulp. Work under water, as seeds are sticky and rinsing helps to clean seeds and separate from pulp.

b.   Spread seeds out on a towel, cloth or screen to dry.

c.   Toss seeds in (vegetable) cooking oil, spread on baking sheet. Bake at 325° until *slightly* browned. Some will "pop" during cooking.

To use the meat of the pumpkin:

a.   Cut and quarter after seeds and pulp are removed.

b.   Bake (325°) sections in a shallow pan with about 1" of water, about 45 minutes, until soft.

c.   Cool. Scrape from shell to use in various recipes.

Pumpkin Pudding (Recipe)

up
↑
3

Mix a cup of puréed pumpkin, sweetened and seasoned as for pie, with a box of vanilla or butterscotch pudding mix. Chill and serve.

Pumpkin Cookies (Recipe)

up
↑
3

2 1/4 cups sifted flour	1/2 cup shortening
1/4 tsp nutmeg	1 1/2 cups sugar
1/2 tsp cinnamon	1 egg
2 1/4 tsps baking powder	1 1/3 cups mashed
1/4 tsp ground cloves	cooked pumpkin

Directions:

Mix dry ingredients together. Blend in shortening, then eggs. Add pumpkin and mix well. Drop by tablespoons onto a baking sheet. Flatten dough slightly with a spoon. Bake in a preheated 375° oven for about 15 minutes or until done. Decorate with orange colored icing and raisin eyes and nose.

Pumpkin Muffins "WINSKY" (Recipe)

up
↑
3

1 egg	1/2 cup sugar
1/2 cup milk	2 tsps baking powder
1/2 cup mashed cooked	1/2 tsp salt
pumpkin	1/2 tsp cinnamon
1/2 cup margarine melted	1/2 tsp nutmeg
1 1/2 cups sifted flour	1/2 cup seedless raisins

Directions:

Beat the eggs slightly with a fork. Stir in milk, pumpkin and margarine. Blend dry ingredients and stir in just until flour is moistened (batter should be lumpy). Fold in raisins. Fill greased muffin tins two-thirds full. Sprinkle 1/4 tsp sugar over each muffin. Bake 18 to 20 minutes at 400°. Makes twelve muffins.

October

up
↑
4

Carrot Shake (Snack, Recipe)

Pour into blender:

    1/4 cup orange juice

    1 tbsp crushed pineapple (apple sauce)

    1/4 cup pineapple juice (apple)

    3 tbsp grated raw carrot

    1 cup whole milk*

Blend to *smooth* consistency. Experiment with other Snack-in-a-Glass combinations of vegetables/fruits. These drinks are high energy, nutritious foods.

Use raw vegetables whenever possible for higher nutritional value. Raw vegetable chunks should be blended smooth to avoid choking hazards.

*Note: Follow local regulations regarding feeding whole or low-fat milk to pre-school age children.

up
↑
4

Healthy Snacks

Develop a poster with children which lists snacks which are high or low in nutrition. Discuss calories, the "fuel" in foods which "burns" and gives our bodies energy. Explain how sweets and sugary foods taste good but provide little nourishment. Remind children about good dental hygiene and to brush after eating, especially sugary foods.

Plus	SNACKS	Minus
apple		candy bar
cantaloupe		Twinkie
celery & peanut butter		Devil Dog
fruit frozen yogurt		chocolate ice cream
carrot sticks		peppermint cane
cherries		marshmallows
graham cracker		chocolate chip cookies

up
↑
2

Cats

Sleek, smooth, graceful! Cats, of all colors, can teach many valuable lessons.

Visit a *dependable* neighborhood cat. *Ask* owner before petting. Ask someone to bring in a gentle cat for a visit. Observe the cat, watch it eat, drink.

Watch the cat wash, stretch, exercise, nap.

up
↑
5

Bats (Pollination)

Read about and show pictures of this mouse-like, flying mammal.

Bats are *very* important to the ecology. They eat hundreds of insects (mosquitos) during nightly feeding flights. They carry pollen from plant-to-plant as they feed.

If—and only if—children express fears about this, assure them that bats *do not* get caught in the hair.

Seed Gatherers (Hibernation)

up ↑ 4

Observe small animals (chipmunks, squirrels, mice, gerbils) and birds. What are they doing as they scurry and flit about? Go to fields, parks and gardens where animals are actively foraging. Examine the plants. Can children find the seeds?

Watch for flocks of ducks and geese. Examine farm gardens where pumpkins, squash and corn have been harvested. Can children find seeds among the old vines and husks?

Butterflies (Ecology, Conservation)

up ↑ 5

Many species of butterflies can be raised. Research those species common to your area. Lure them by the plants they prefer. Consult nature guides for pictures and other information.

Teach children that butterflies need protection and help them raise and preserve them.

MONARCH BUTTERFLY

1.   Look for the chrysalis attached to milkweed plants.

2.   Collect, keeping on plants, and place in a container (jar, small box) covered with screen.

3.   Watch for emerging butterfly. When butterflies hatch, feed with sugar-water solution.

4.   Release outside when the butterflies are active and ready to fly.

Leaves

up ↑ 5

Deciduous trees are those which shed their leaves in autumn, such as maple, oak, birch, beech, etc. It isn't necessary for children to identify them by name, but it sharpens their observational skills to look for the differences in the bark, the shapes of the leaves, and the shape of the tree.

Besides looking to see how many different trees they can find, they can:

• Make bark rubbings.

• Put leaves between two sheets of paper and make rubbings.

• Dig into a compost of leaves to observe the decay process.

• Dig into woodland humus to observe black "soil" forming.

Gourds

up ↑ 5

Gourds grow in a fascinating array of colors, shapes, sizes and textures. Many projects are possible, such as musical instruments, bird houses, puppets.

Although they resemble squash and pumpkins, gourds are inedible.

Small gourds make excellent maracas. Select a pair with natural handles. Be sure that the gourds are dry. Cut the gourds open crosswise toward the bottom and scrape out the seeds and pith. Put in some coarse gravel or tiny pebbles. Glue the two sections together and shellac.

October

Milkweed

^{up} ↑ 2

Collect pods, one for each child. Open pods, pull apart seeds. Blow them and watch the wind carry them away.

Ask: "How are pumpkin and milkweed seeds protected?" (Apple seeds? Orange seeds?)

Place some pods in clear plastic bags. Observe daily to watch for changes as pods dry and seeds burst out.

Pumpkin to Compost

^{up} ↑ 4

When you carve a Jack-o-Lantern for display, put it outside following Halloween celebrations. Watch the decaying process as the shell collapses, molds and rots.

Draw pictures of the changing faces of the collapsing pumpkin.

Place a whole, uncut pumpkin beside the hollow one to observe differences.

Bury the rotted shells and explain their value as compost.

Touch and Feel Boxes (Sensory)

5 ↑ 3

Cover large/small, round/square/oblong boxes with a variety of textures. Put assorted texture items inside. Make some all the same, i.e. soft/furry surfaces with soft items inside, or scratchy/rough surfaces mixed with smooth ones. Use:

CLOTH	PAPER & PLASTIC	INSIDE ITEMS
burlap	paper towel	cotton balls
corduroy	corrugated cardboard	screws
denim	crêpe paper	erasers
satin	construction paper	yarn/string
felt	tissue	balls (tennis, etc.)
leather	foil	shells
gauze	sandpaper	wood-scraps
velvet	plastic wrap	candles

- Children guess, mix and match textures, sort. Expand vocabulary with as many descriptive words as possible.

- Cut small, hand-sized holes around the sides of a large carton. Cut "wrists" off work gloves (or sock tops) and attach around holes. Children reach through cloth openings to feel and identify various objects. Ask such questions as:

  "Can you feel and take out two round objects and one flat one?"

  "How many rough things can you touch?"

MUSIC—MOVEMENT

Baby Seeds

5 ↑ 3

Use the poem to conduct a creative movement session.

In a milkweed cradle	Open wide the cradle
Snug and warm	Hold it high
Baby seeds hiding	Come Mr. Wind
Safe and warm	Help them fly.

(Author unknown)

[5↑3] *Mouse and Pumpkin (Stories)*

Read *Mousekin's Golden House* by Edna Miller (pub. Scholastic). Use the story to develop different kinds of movement. Use silent mime. Choose music to accompany motions. Suggestions:

- Seeds and cranberries pop on ground.
- Cat creeps slowly.
- Owl swoops.
- "Mousekin" jumps in pumpkin's mouth.
- Wind whistles, snow blows.
- Pumpkin doors settle lower.
- "Mousekin" sleeps.

[5↑2] *Pumpkins to Jack-O-Lanterns*

- Be pumpkins! Start as seeds; grow into vines and pumpkins; grow bigger and rounder. Pumpkins roll, vines creep and crawl.
- Add orange and green scarves to "pumpkins" and "vines."
- Use hands and fingers only. Carve, scoop and light an imaginary Jack-o-Lantern.

TODDLERS, TOO!

[up↑3] *Pumpkin, Pumpkin*

The following song can be used as you draw a face on a pumpkin with a black magic marker.

> *Pumpkin, pumpkin, yellow pumpkin,*
> *Pumpkin, pumpkin, yellow pumpkin,*
> *Pumpkin, pumpkin, yellow pumpkin,*
> *Heigh, ho, pumpkin!*

2nd verse—*Give him a smile like a silly-sally sumpkin.*

3rd verse—*Give him a nose like a nilly-nally numpkin.*

4th verse—*Give him some eyes like an illy-ally umpkin.*

5th verse—*Pumpkin, pumpkin, Halloween pumpkin.*

[5↑3] *Firefighters at Work*

Develop a movement session around firefighter's duty. The firefighter is sleeping. Alarm! Jumps out of bed into clothes, pulls on boots, slides down pole, runs to truck, drives to fire, pulls hose, sprays water, climbs ladder, rescues people, puts on mask to go inside, returns to station, polishes truck, etc.

No more fires, the engines are back in their barns and all the equipment is polished and put away. The firefighters climb out of their heavy boots, hang up their slickers and hats and go to their beds to rest.

LANGUAGE—DRAMA

up
↑
5

Messages (Listening Skills)

- Develop concentration skills with oral language. Give directions, gradually increasing in difficulty.

    For example: "Bring two square blocks." Then: "Bring two square blocks, put them behind Sarah." Then: "Bring two square blocks, put them behind Sarah, tell her to take one to José."

- Take one child aside. Give a message to be repeated to the group. Increase difficulty. "The wind is blowing today." "The wind is blowing today and the sun is shining."

5
↑
3

The Boat—It Happened!

Kathy, age three and a half, came into school with a boat magazine. Her teacher sat beside her and together they looked at the pictures and talked about them. Several other children joined them and the teacher asked, "Would you like to make a boat?"

"Let's make a sailboat. My daddy has a boat just like this one in the picture," replied Kathy.

Four sheets of brown construction paper were taped together and children defined the shape of the boat with crayons and cut it out. They asked for white paper and made a sail.

On another day, as the children looked at the boat pictures, the teacher asked, "What makes the boats stay on top of the water?" The children searched the room, testing different articles to see which would float and which would sink. The teacher made a list of 'sinkers' and 'floaters' and hung it on the wall over the sink.

One day the children came to school and found a refrigerator carton on the floor. Their teacher had drawn an oval in black crayon on the side. "It's a boat!" exclaimed the first child to arrive. Soon several were cutting out the center with large shears. This was hard work for threes but the teacher was amazed that she had to give very little help. Their enthusiasm carried them along during this difficult manipulative task.

"Can we paint our boat?" they came to ask.

The following day the boat was set on newspapers and large brushes and cans of paint laid out. "What color do you want?" As might be expected, several colors were requested. Everyone had a turn and the completed boat was decorated in designs of many colors.

For several days the boat was the center of dramatic play as the children climbed in and out, chattering, sailing, taking trips, fixing, fishing.

Then one morning the children found a full-sized set of oars standing in a corner. "Oars. I know what they're for. We have them in our boat," exclaimed George.

It took a lot of *cooperative* effort and *problem solving* to get the long, heavy oars to the boat in the center of the floor. Seat blocks were placed on either side of the 'cockpit' and two inside. With two children holding on inside, the oars resting on the sides of the boat and others holding on, it became almost real.

The children sang *Row, Row, Row Your Boat* and *Michael Row the Boat Ashore*. With this came the highlight of the whole adventure. Michael, a shy three, had been slow to adjust to school and had never really become involved in any of the groups' activities. He was always an onlooker. But when he heard them singing *his* name, he grinned from ear to ear. They were singing about him—to him. He was IN!

(All this happened spontaneously. How tragic it would have been if some overly conscientious teacher had said, "We can't 'do' boats now. It is October and we will 'do' Halloween.")

CREATIVE PROJECTS

5 ↑ 3 *Tree Mural*

Paint blues and greens of various shades onto newspapers. Dry. Tear into long 6"-8" wide strips. Paste to long mural to create sky/water/earth. Add torn paper white clouds and brown paper hills.

Cut black/brown tree trunks and limbs with many branches.

Children dip palms into various autumn leaf shades and print hand-leaves onto the mural.

5 ↑ 3 *Arm Trees*

Trace around arm and hand of child. The arm is the trunk, the fingers are the branches. Sponge paint bright leaves onto "finger" branches.

MASKS

Young children are often afraid to wear masks over their faces, or find them uncomfortable. Paper plates decorated with faces and held in front on sticks can serve as well.

---

up ↑ 5 *Paper Plate Masks*

Punch holes into top and side edges of a paper plate. Lace yarn hair through holes or staple torn paper/cloth strips around edges for hair.

Glue on facial features. Attach to stick to hold in front of face. Older children might make these for younger children as an after school project.

up ↑ 4 *T-Shirt and Paper Bag Costumes*

Decorated, fringed, tie-died T-shirts and large paper bags are simple, easy-to-wear costumes.

Add several layers of fringed cloth/paper to create animal fur or feather effects.

Paper Bag Vest

up ↑ 3 *Ghosts/Puppets*

- Cut luncheon plate size circles of cloth. Put cotton balls or wad of cloth in the center and attach to sticks or straight clothespins with ties or elastics. Draw on a face.

- Tie tissues to fingers for instant ghosts. Compose "This little ghost" rhymes and counting games.

- Fold white paper. Cut 1/2 of ghost silhouette (see illustration). Punch eye hole. Cut mouth. Unfold and paste on black.

HC

October

up ↑ 5 ### *Halloween Mural*
Draw landscape features (horizon, hills, water, land) onto mural paper. Fill in with paint and/or scraps . Add silhouettes of trees. Ask children to draw/dress paper doll figures of themselves and place in mural scene. Add tiny pumpkins, cats, bats, ghosts, skeletons and scarecrows.

TODDLERS might add Halloween stickers and put star stickers into the night sky.

Encourage story telling based on the scene.

up ↑ 5 ### *My Skeleton*
Cut white paper into 1" strips and a circle (head). Build a skeleton by pasting pieces (bones) on a large sheet of black paper. (Sheets of newsprint painted black will also serve for background.)

Masking tape strips can also be used for bones.

Children feel for, count and name bones on their bodies as they build skeletons.

JUST FOR FUN

up ↑ 4 ### *Engine House*
Make fire stations painting small cartons/shoe boxes red!

Mark each box with a numeral (1 to 10).

Mark same numerals on 10 small vehicles. Ask children to drive the correct engine into its station.

up ↑ 4 ### *Pocketbook/Coupon Game (Sets)*
- Mount matching sets of trading/discount coupons on cardboard, or, cut coupons/logos/brand names from boxes. (Cereal, jello, milk, noodles)
- Place matching set of products (or coupons) on "store" shelves.
- Put three to eight coupons into pocket books.
- Children go shopping for products which match their "list" of coupons.

up ↑ 5 ### *Facial Expressions (Emotions)*
- Older children cut facial features from magazines.
- Sort into categories—eyes, noses, etc.
- Assemble faces on paper circles or plates.
- Ask children to make "happy," "sad," "angry," etc. faces.

up ↑ 2 ### *Pumpkin Toss*
Cut a large pumpkin shape from cardboard. Cut out *large* holes for features. Paint orange (TODDLERS) and prop it against a wall.

Toss bean bags or balls through the eyes, nose, and mouth. Five's and older children may like to keep score: Eyes—5 points, Nose—10 points, etc.

SEQUENCE THREE

NOVEMBER

NOVEMBER THEMES

NOVEMBER

Grandpa and the "Hokey Pokey"

Children in a mobile society miss the opportunity to establish close relationships with **relatives** beyond their immediate family. **Thanksgiving** is often a time for l**arge family gatherings.** **Grandparents, aunts, uncles** and **cousins** visit—an entire **family tree** of company! As we prepare for **guests**, we teach children a few simple ideas about **hosting** and good manners by our examples.

Native Americans shared squash, **cranberries, baked beans** and **corn bread** with their **Mayflower hosts.** At later Thanksgiving **feasts, ancestors** traveled by **horse** and wagon—"over the river and through the woods." Today's guests use many kinds of **transportation**—planes, trains, buses, ships, automobiles.

Candidates campaign for November **elections**, hoping to convince **voters** to choose them at **polling places.** Children can learn how to **make choices** and **discuss issues** at **meetings.** **Native Americans** used **drum talk** and **tribal symbols** at **pow wows** and still come together at **potlatches** and tribal councils.

Children add to their **daily successes in child care** during November as they practice **left/ right** concepts in the **"Hokey-Pokey"**; find **squares, rectangles** and **cubes**; make **linear measurements**; learn about **cornucopias** and **thankfulness**; and discover **autumn colors.**

Native Americans introduced **corn** to the **Pilgrims.** Their tribal "cousins" in Mexico, Central and South America still use **maize (corn flour)** to bake **tortillas.**

During autumn farmers store **vegetables** and **grain harvests; squirrels, chipmunks** gather and store seeds; **ducks** and **geese flock** and **migrate.**

Children can trace around hands to make a **family tree** or a **turkey.** They can create **place mats** for **harvest tables** and decorate **Indian costumes** with crêpe paper dye and **plaster medallions.** What is your **tribal name**? How many ways can you use **descriptive language** to tell about **painting day surprises**?

Will you ride a **hobby horse** on a **nut hunt** or follow **arrows**—JUST FOR FUN?

SEQUENCE THREE

PEOPLE

5 ↑ 3 *Family Tree*

During lunch/snack and other discussion times, ask, "Who is in your family besides your parents?" "Do you have grandparents?" (Uncles? Cousins?) "Can you name them?" "Who is coming to visit during the holidays?" "Who sends you special cards/gifts on your birthday?"

Trace around each child's hand and write the names of family groups on the fingers (limbs).

Write parents' names on the palm (trunk) and grandparents' names on the wrist (roots).

5 ↑ 3 *Grandparents*

Ask: "Who does Dad/Mom call 'Daddy'/'Mom'?" "Who took your Dad to the dentist?" "Who helped your Mom with her homework?"

"What do you call your grandparents?" (List all the nicknames for grandparents.)

Discuss relative age differences, i.e. grandparents are the oldest, parents come next in age, then children.

Sort family groups into two categories. Discuss: "Who are the adults?" "Children?" Then point out that adults were also the children once.

up ↑ 5 *Origins*

Invite parents/grandparents to visit and tell about origins.

Show pictures and add other information about places of origin, how families came to America (if immigrants).

List the different countries, languages, ethnic groups, tribal names.

Ask children to draw pictures of grandparents.

EXPANDING OUR WORLD

In naming different ethnic groups, we have attempted to be sensitive to current acceptable usage of terms for those groups. Ask the parents their preferences and teach the words to the children when describing people.

up ↑ 5 *Pilgrims and Native Americans/Indians*

Pilgrims were people who came to America from England a long time ago—before telephones and electric lights and cars and planes. They came on a ship called the Mayflower which didn't even have an engine—it moved by sail—so it took them a long time to get here.

We call the Indians Native Americans because they were here *before* people came from countries like England. Early explorers called them Indians because they thought they had reached India.

Explore with the children the following questions.

- Do you think there were people waiting to meet them? Hotels where they could sleep?
- They had used up almost all the food they had on the ship. Could they buy more?
- It was almost winter. Could they plant a garden to get food? Who do you think helped them that first winter?

Transportation Depots/Stations

Ask: "How many different ways do people travel to the center?" "How many ways can people travel to come to America?"

Show pictures (travel brochures) of ships, planes, trains, busses. "Who has ridden in each one?" "How did your family travel to America?"

- "What is it like to ride on a bus?" "What (how) do you eat?" "Go to sleep?"
- "Where do you sit on an airplane?" "Where is the bathroom?"

Explore each way of traveling. Role play BUS/TRAIN/SHIP, etc.

Visit a station, depot, airport. Look for ticket booths, restaurants, baggage areas, taxi stands, toilets.

Stable/Horse

Visit a stable or farm.

Horses are used for transportation. How else are they used? How do they sleep? Keep warm? City children may be able to see horses at a Mounted Police Unit.

What do horses eat that people eat? Ask the owner to feed a crunchy apple or carrot so the children can hear the chewing.

Listen to a horse drinking.

Look at the horse's tongue and teeth. Compare with a cat's tongue and teeth.

Elections (Math, Names)

Talk about election activities. Show newspaper pictures of people who are candidates.

Provide opportunities for children to "vote" for choices at "meetings" and discussions.

To demonstrate how real elections work:

- Make ballot boxes and ballots. Make a voting booth—a large carton or puppet theater with a curtain.
- Decide on an issue. For example, vote for round or square cracker at snack time. Children vote by dropping round or square shapes into the ballot box. Stress the fact that only the shape with the *most votes* will be served that day—*majority* wins!

Polling Places

Schools, town/city halls, mobile units have voting machines and booths. Arrange to visit one. "Why do they have curtains?" "Who can use them?"

"Do you have to put coins into the machines to make them work?" "Why can't children vote?"

SKILLS FOR DAILY LIVING

Daily Successes in Child Care

Keep books/charts recording "I CAN!" at school. Praise and show approval DAILY and OFTEN.

Try these: GOOD! HOORAY! FANTASTIC! GREAT JOB! ALL BY YOURSELF! WITHOUT ANY HELP! BUENO! GUTE! WAY TO GO!

Picture	I CAN!
Pitcher	Pour, no spills!
Scissors	Cut on a line
Name tag	Write my name (or find my cubby)
Hand/smiling face	"Say Goodbye" no tears
Blocks	Clean up my toys
Water faucet	Turn off (save) water

Table Setting

- Make placemats showing the placement of fork, knife, spoon, glass and napkin.

- Children lay out the placemats, using chairs as a guide.

- Children then put eating utensils, etc. on the mats.

Meetings/Pow-wows (Multi-cultural, Routines)

During the first weeks of child care, a group of children (3's and up) will need a time together to discuss, plan, establish rules and routines. This gathering together need not be at the very beginning of the day, but rather after most have arrived so care givers can explain daily schedule and talk about other concerns.

"MEETINGS" may be called for special/emergency/"ad-hoc" announcements. For example:

- "Julie fell near the sink and got a bad bruise. The floor was wet and very slippery. What can we do to prevent this from happening?" (Clean/dry the floor.)

- Supplies were used up before a **special activity** could be done by the entire group. "How can we solve this problem?" (Be careful not to waste things.)

- The center has become very noisy, children are disruptive and some are crying, screaming, wrestling, or hitting. ("STOP! We need a meeting.")

Be careful that "**gatherings**" (regular daily meetings) do not become stale and boring. Keep them fresh, with surprises and unexpected moments. "**Circle Time**" has too often become an "activity" to be "gotten through."

Note: Native Americans held "Pow-wows" and "Potlatches" to discuss ideas. You may wish to use these names to refresh your gathering times. Change the location, sit on a special blanket, build a make-believe campfire and sit around it, elect chiefs (tribal leaders) and divide into tribes for activities.

CONCEPTS

<table>
<tr><td>5
↑
3</td><td></td></tr>
</table>

Left//Right

When teaching these concepts, use the words "correct," "good," or "fine" instead of "right" to avoid confusion.

When helping with shoes/boots, always *squeeze* the right foot and *point* to the left foot. (Say, "I squeeze the *right* and point to the *left*.) The same with mittens and sleeves.

Autumn Colors (Mural)

Collect leaves and grasses and arrange from darkest shades to the lightest. Look especially for the purple/maroon leaves for the darkest hue. Use grass stalks laid side-by-side to create the pale shades of cream to brown.

- Draw a giant leaf shape on mural paper. Fill the leaf from dark to light using the natural colors of leaves and grasses.

- Color patches of paper and take them outside to find natural color matches.

- Divide a paper into three to six sections. Put a color patch in each section, include greys, browns, and black. Use photographs in magazines. Ask children to find natural objects of the same colors. Be *fussy*—ask for a close match.

Squares/Rectangles/Cubes (Math, Sets)

Look for and list objects in these shapes. Use rulers to determine the differences.

Put out an assortment of square boxes, from a large carton to a tiny box. Ask children to fit them all together. How high can the boxes be stacked? Measure the differences between the stack and the nested boxes.

Ask children to lay the boxes (cubes) out in a line from smallest to largest. Measure. (If the boxes are square, the vertical stack and the horizontal row should be the same.) Use the words "vertical" and "horizontal" during measuring activities.

After block play, ask one group to store blocks in neat unit divisions. Ask another group to pile the same amount of blocks in a "helter-skelter" way. Ask which is better and why.

Point-to-Point (Geometric Shapes, Math)

Use large string or elastic loops to stretch triangles, rectangles, squares from various points (table legs, door knobs, hooks) across an area. Ask one child to use two, three and four children as "pointers" by standing on string/elastic loops or holding it.

Place 6, 8, etc. children at equal distances and create geometric shapes—squares, hexagons, octagons, etc.

SCHOOL AGE

Cornucopia/Conch/Shells

Use this unusual shape to introduce and *enjoy* the sound of the word "cornucopia"—a symbol for "abundance." Children might look for the symbol in holiday displays. Early people used scallop shells as scoops and conch shells as horns. Experiment with scooping and measuring using various shells.

Wet sand and press shell patterns into it. Use small, spoon-sized shells to scoop mashed potatoes/pudding at a Pilgrim/Native American feast.

Note: *Conch* is usually pronounced "conk," like "honk."

SCIENCE

Corn Meal, Flour/Bread (Nutrition)
up ↑ 4

Settlers, Pilgrims, Native tribes and "old time" people raised and ground their own grains into flour.

Seed corn kernels can be pounded into coarse meal, and corn meal pounded into flour.

Experiment by using rounded stones (pestles) and hollows in flat rocks (mortars). CAUTION: Do not use metal hammers as rocks easily chip.

A wooden meat hammer and a *sturdy* wooden salad bowl may also serve.

Pound a small amount of meal or flour. Compare with commercial products.

Mix with a small amount of water into a paste. Taste. Repeat using prepared flour.

Use a mix, or bake from scratch, some corn muffins/bread.

Tortillas/Corn Chips (Multi-Cultural)
up ↑ 3

Offer samples of various corn products for tasting and smelling.

These foods are commonly used by Hispanic Americans. Invite parents of Hispanic children to prepare other foods using corn flour, possibly show the process of making tortillas.

What other ethnic breads are used by families who use the center?

Serve vegetable purées as dips with corn chips.

Yeast Breads (Stories)
up ↑ 4

Make yeast bread, and while dough rises, read *The Duchess Bakes A Cake* by Virginia Kahl (pub. Scribner). Making yeast bread involves mixing, rising, punching, rising, baking and then EATING. Especially good activity for children who stay all day.

Cranberries
up ↑ 3

Show pictures of bogs and plants.

Cook and serve as sauce/jelly, over ice cream, in breads/cakes. Compare jelly with jello.

Weigh uncooked berries before and after cooking. Weigh, also, any ingredients (water/sugar) added to the cranberries.

Baked Beans (Math, Multi-cultural)
up ↑ 5

Choose two or three kinds of beans—pea, kidney, yellow eye, black—to prepare in different batches for baking. Involve children in the entire process from inspection for stones, washing, soaking, parboiling, draining and seasoning, to baking. This is a two-day+ process.

Serve cooked beans in a variety of ways, for example mash and re-fry as in Hispanic-American cultures. Scoop beans with corn chips and roll them into tortillas.

Make bean soup from combinations of beans, rice and vegetables (combining beans with rice enhances the nutritional content of both.)

At each stage of preparation discuss smell, taste, texture and color. What happens to the size and volume of beans?

up ↑ 4 *Squirrels/Chipmunks (Gatherers)*

Watch these animals at work. What are they doing? Why? What do they eat? Go to a spot under a nut or cone bearing tree (oak, hickory, chestnut, pine) and look for "evidence" (shells). Watch the routes the animal uses going to and from a food source, especially a chipmunk. Try to find the entrance hole to a nest.

Put some seeds, berries, grapes where a chipmunk might come. Watch as the cheek pouches fill up as the animal gathers food to carry it to the nest.

Compare with pets such as gerbils/hamsters. How are they alike or different?

What do these animals do that people do to have a supply of food? Look in the kitchen cupboards and refrigerator for stored foods.

Early tribes gathered and stored foods for winter use. Why? How? (See July—SCIENCE— *Dried and Dehydrated Foods*)

up ↑ 4 *Ducks/Geese (Migration)*

Watch for flocking ducks and geese as they gather to graze and migrate. Some will stay all winter. They have come from more northern areas; others leave your area and fly farther south.

What do they eat? Look in a squash, pumpkin or corn field for "evidence." Follow duck tracks in the mud at the edge of a pond. Look at the crisscross patterns. Later, after a snowfall, return to see if ducks are still living there.

Watch for V-shaped flocks of migrating ducks or geese. Ask: "Why do they fly in a 'V'?" (Shape causes an "airfoil" effect, similar to an airplane.)

up ↑ 4 *Vegetable Garden Chart*

Show many kinds of vegetables (or use pictures). Discuss which grow above ground and which grow under ground.

Read *Up Above and Down Below* by Irma E. Webber (pub. Young Scott Books), in connection with this activity.

Look in magazines and seed catalogs for colored photographs of vegetables. "Plant" a vegetable garden by taping two cardboard strips across poster board to make pockets to hold vegetable pictures. Label top strip "above ground" and bottom strip "below ground." Put pictures of beets, potatoes, carrots, etc. in underground pockets, and beans, lettuce, celery, etc. in above ground pockets.

HARVEST MURAL

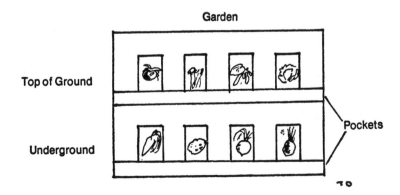

up ↑ 3 *Smell Hunt*

Hide an onion which has been cut in half; spray a corner of the room with perfume; spread coffee grounds in a corner; put some orange slices under a cloth; conceal a cake of scented soap; put some chocolate under a cloth.

Send children on a smelling hunt. As each scent is located, child returns to tell teacher the location. Remind—don't point or tell the place to others, whisper it to the teacher.

up ↑ 4 *What Have I Here? (Touch, Language Skills)*

Put four to six objects into a bag or box. Put identical objects into another bag or box. Child feels and describes an object but does not name it or remove it.

Another child finds the matching object in second bag using the description given.

Encourage use of many adjectives for size, shape, texture and other attributes.

up ↑ 5 *Linear Measure (Math)*

Children measure a table top using unit blocks. Record: "The table is 10 blocks long and 4 blocks wide." Then, use real measuring tool (tape measures or rulers) to re-measure the same table. Discuss the advantages of using real rulers.

- Use a child's "toe-heel" measurement for a room. Compare with the same method done by an adult. What was the difference? Ask the same two to use a tape measure and compare results.

- Talk about and show ruler markings and sizes, i.e. inches, feet, yards, meters.

- Explain how earlier people used their feet, strides, knuckles, and hands as measuring devices.

- Ask a mounted policeman (or horse owner) to demonstrate "spans" when measuring animals.

SCHOOL AGE

MUSIC—MOVEMENT

up ↑ 5 *Rhythm Patterns (Reading Readiness)*

Make and cut hand and foot patterns by tracing around hands and feet (or shoes) on heavy paper. Punch hanging holes. Hand = "clap" and foot = "stamp."

Use arrangements of hand/foot patterns to indicate rhythms, to clap/stamp. Children "compose" rhythmic exercises by setting up patterns in various combinations.

up ↑ 4 *Transportation Sounds*

Use records/tapes (available from libraries) of sound effects to accompany this activity, or make up tapes "on location" of real boat (plane, truck, subway, motorcycle) sounds.

Use sandpaper blocks, sticks, bells and vocal effects to simulate sounds.

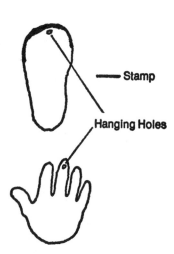

Stamp

Hanging Holes

Arrange Cut-Outs to Make "Composition"

Ten Little Indians (Counting Song)

Sing this traditional song, changing words to count "Pilgrims," "pumpkins," "turkeys," etc.

Make finger puppets using toothpaste caps. Glue acorns into the depression on top.

Decorate plastic thimbles and small (not too tight!) pill bottles with faces, hair and hats.

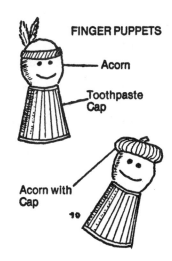

FINGER PUPPETS

Acorn

Toothpaste Cap

Acorn with Cap

Hunter's Walk (Listening Skills, Group Control, Transitions)

Describe a person and the action and ask children to mime the action, for example:

"Native Americans are going through the woods hunting. They wear soft moccasins. (Take off shoes.) They must avoid stepping on twigs which snap. (Scatter some twigs.) They must push overhanging branches aside quietly. There is a stream with slippery stepping stones and a steep, muddy bank..."

Do this activity *outside* on different surfaces (woods, gravel, pavement, high grass). Divide into two groups. One group is blindfolded and stands at points along the route. The second group walks, trying to avoid being heard.

Listeners wave a flag if they hear a walker pass by. (No talking, very quiet, *listening* activity!)

Drums (Musical Instruments)

Hoop Drum

Use *heavy* cardboard tubes and plastic drain pipe sections for drums. Stretch inner tubing, leather, canvas, nylon or plastic over openings.

Tom-Tom

Use hollow logs, metal and plastic containers to create a variety of sounds.

Hand-Drums

Coffee, juice and other cans with plastic covers make drums. Experiment with various drumsticks to create sharp-to-muffled beats. Attach bead strings to outside for "rattle" effect. Attach shoulder strap so child can march while drumming.

Paint and decorate drums (and other homemade instruments) with beads, feathers, designs, cloth patches, buttons, etc. Train children to treat all instruments carefully and store in safe places after using. (See August—MUSIC—MOVEMENT—*Homemade Instruments*)

Plastic Drain Pipe

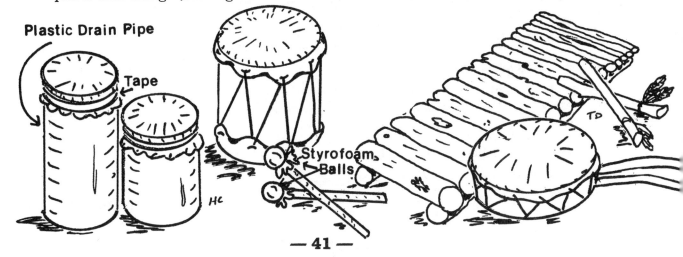

Tape

Styrofoam Balls

Drum Talk (Rhythmic Patterns, Listening)

up ↑ 4

One person beats a rhythm, others answer. Patterns become more intricate as activity progresses.

One person goes to another room or behind a curtain and sends a drum "message," others respond, then send a different "message" in return.

Older children might set up "Morse code" style messages, i.e.

One tap—hello

Two taps—goodbye

Three taps—juice time

Two-plus one—come back

Elastic Loops

up ↑ 5

Use 1/2" dressmaker's elastic sewn into loops (about five yards). Explore motions with the loops.

Stand in a circle with everyone holding the elastic. Change the shape by moving about while holding on.

Make sounds by plucking the loop, stretched to various lengths, between holders.

Toe, Knee, Chest, Nut (Game, Group Control)

up ↑ 3

Toe, knee, chest, nut

(Touch toes, touch knees,

touch chest, touch head)

Toe, knee, chest, nut

(Repeat movements)

I love you

(Touch eyes, cross arms over

chest, point to child)

I love you

(Repeat movements)   (Gradually say the words faster so
                             it sounds like *Tony Chestnut!*)

Hokey-Pokey (Left/Right)

5 ↑ 3

Use this familiar song to teach left/right concepts.

You put your right hand in, you put your right hand out.

You put your right hand in, and you shake it all about.

You do the Hokey-Pokey and you turn yourself around.

That's what it's all about.

Repeat, changing words to: foot, head, shoulder, elbow, etc. End with:

You put your whole self in, you put your whole self out,

You put your whole self in, and you shake it all about,

You do the Hokey-Pokey and you turn yourself around.

That's what it's all about.

LANGUAGE—DRAMA

up ↑ 4

Travel Posters (Extended Family, Collage, Story-telling)

Discuss places where grandparents (and other relatives/friends) live—especially those who are coming to visit or where children will go on vacations and visits.

What is the climate? What grows there? How do people travel? What are houses/buildings like?

Choose three or four places to "visit." Groups of children collect pictures for each location and make collages for travel posters.

Children also make up individual posters about places where relatives live or where they travel.

Use posters in story-telling: "My uncle Aaron lives in Chicago. He is coming by bus to visit."

Take imaginary trips. Stimulate, dramatize, play with rows of seats, tickets, suitcases, schedules and sound effects.

up ↑ 4

Autumn (Language Skills)

Ask children: "What does the word *Autumn* make you think of?" Develop activities around these autumn themes. Some examples:

General

Colored leaves	Indians	Storing nuts
Thanksgiving	Feathers	Squirrels
Turkey	Migration	Pine needles
Pilgrims	Harvest	Chilly
Mayflower	Hibernation	Fog

Hibernation

Animals gathering food	Insulation (fur, what keeps a house warm?)
People gathering food	Gathering seeds
Tunnels	Classifying things (floaters, stickers, animals)
Bears in caves	Cocoons and butterflies

Migration

Birds	Maps	Gathering seeds
Climates and seasons	Flocking	Traveling
Feeding winter birds	Bird feeders	Flying and planes

Frost

Lacy pictures	Ice	Storm windows
Condensation	First snow flurries	Mittens and hats
Lace doilies	Bringing plants inside	Breathing on glass

up ↑ 4

Thankfulness (Language Skills, Books)

Ask children "Why do you say 'Thank you'? What makes you thankful?" Make books with their responses. Add pictures and drawings which illustrate "I am Thankful."

Native American Tribal Names/Symbols

up ↑ 4

Divide into tribes. Choose names for tribes and individuals based upon descriptive characteristics of each child, for instance:

"Melyssa found the lost puzzle pieces, she's—GOOD HUNTER."

"Shideh is the tallest—he is CLOUD TOUCHER."

"Alyson has a quiet (soft) voice—her name is WHISPERING ONE."

"Dana always paints with red—RED PAINTER."

"Anna has long, long braids—ANNA LONG BRAIDS."

Choose tribal names, colors and symbols. Make badges and paint T-shirts with symbols on them.

Tribes come together for pow-wows and potlatches. They divide into tribes for smaller group activities and games.

NATIVE AMERICAN SYMBOLS

 = 4 AGES—INFANCY, YOUTH, MIDDLE AGE, OLD AGE

 = MAN—HUMAN LIFE

 = SNAKE—DEFIANCE

 = BROKEN ARROW—PEACE

 = CACTUS FLOWER—LOVE

 = CROSSED ARROWS—FRIENDSHIP

 = TEEPEE—TEMPORARY HOME

 = SUN SYMBOLS—HAPPINESS

 = HEADDRESS—CEREMONIAL DANCE

 = BIRD—CAREFREE, LIGHTHEARTED

 = ENCLOSURE FOR CEREMONIAL DANCE

 = BUTTERFLY—EVERLASTING LIFE

 = DEER TRACK—PLENTY GAME

 = RATTLESNAKE JAW—STRENGTH

 = RAIN CLOUD—GOOD PROSPECTS

 = SUN'S RAYS—TRUTH

 = RAINDROP/RAIN—PLENTIFUL CROPS

= BIG MOUNTAIN—ABUNDANCE

= MORNING STARS—GUIDANCE

7D

Descriptive Language (Adjectives/Adverbs)

Show pictures of flowers, foods, scenes, children, animals, etc. Ask children to describe using one word. Write the words on a large poster. Try to think of other words which are more descriptive. Keep poster up and add words as they occur in stories, or general conversation.

CREATIVE PROJECTS

 Hands Tree (Mural)

Paint a large tree shape on mural-sized paper. Draw a branch for each child to name family members. Trace around child's hand to make "leaves," one for each family member. Child puts the leaves on the family branch.

Turkey Hands/Mural

- Trace around child's open hand to make the body of a turkey. Color finger "feathers" bright colors, add a turkey head.

- Make a large mural using many hand tracings in autumn colors as turkey feathers.

Badges/Medallions/Wampum

To make badges and medallions, drop rounds of plaster of paris on waxed paper. Make a hole for stringing. Dry. Decorate with acrylic paint.

String seashells which have natural stringing holes.

Use medallions and shells in trading games as native tribes used wampum for money.

Harvest Table (Sets, Spatial Relations, Family)

Use shoe boxes (or similar) as tables. Child pastes circles (plates) around edges, one for each family member at a holiday dinner.

Cut slits just large enough to hold tongue depressors (people). Slits (chairs) are matched with plates.

Draw faces on depressors, representing each family member. Child seats family around the table, putting stick family into the slits.

Ask: "Who sits beside...?" "Across from...?" "To the right (left) of...?"

Children play games "Who's coming to dinner?" Invite another child's family; combine families and double tables.

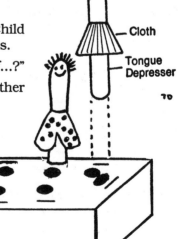

Yarn

Cloth

Tongue
Depresser

Who Lives at My House?

up ↑ 4

Cut house shapes from cardboard, one for each child. Cut a door flap and two or three window openings. Attach pockets to the back of the house under the windows.

Use the stick dolls from previous activity to put "my family" in the windows by slipping them into the pockets.

"Who is upstairs, down, etc." Make animal stick figures to represent pets.

Children pretend to visit each other's homes. "Who is at home?" "Which room is yours?" Ask: "Can you put the mother in the top window?"

Crêpe Paper Dye

5 ↑ 3

Stretch a white cloth (sheet or *cotton* curtain) over a fence or lay on a paved area. Dip crêpe paper streamers in water and lay on the cloth. Create designs by crisscrossing/overlaying the paper so colors will bleed into each other.

Use the cloth for feasts, a stage curtain and other special activities.

Placemats (Spray/Spatter Paint)

up ↑ 3

Arrange grasses, leaves, feathers, pine spills, shells, flower petals on sheets of construction paper. Spray or spatter paint over arrangements. When paint dries, remove arrangements.

JUST FOR FUN

Stand-Up Costumes

up ↑ 3

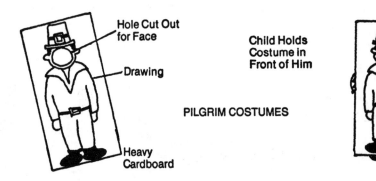

Hole Cut Out for Face

Drawing

Heavy Cardboard

Child Holds Costume in Front of Him

PILGRIM COSTUMES

Painting Day—Surprise!

up ↑ 2

Put away all activities except paints and related equipment (sponges, printers, brushes, feathers, rollers, etc.).

Set up areas inside and outside, offering a different technique in each area. Encourage children to try new things.

Invite parents to participate.

Display all the creations at an exhibit.

Serve "fancy" refreshments on lace doilies.

Nut Hunt (Math, Sets, Seriation)

up ↑ 4

Hide an assortment of nuts, inside and outside on different days. Children hunt in teams or alone in assigned areas.

Count and sort into categories. If nuts and variety are counted before hiding, teams can go back and search for —"two more brazil nuts," "five more acorns," "one more almond."

Hobby Horses

up ↑ 5

Make heads from suggestions below and attach to sturdy stick or dowel. (Use discarded tool and broom handles.)

a)   *Man's sock* stuffed—add fringed cloth or yarn mane and button eyes and nostrils.

b)   *Paper bag* stuffed—add paper fringe and features.

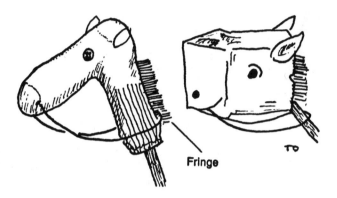

Fringe

Arrows (Game, Spatial Concepts, Left/Right)

up ↑ 4

•   Set up a path or obstacle course with various large muscle activities. Make up cards with arrows and lay out along the course. Children follow the direction indicated.

•   Use arrows to lay out paths. Children follow the arrows to the surprise destination, i.e. snacks set out on a blanket, a new activity center or game.

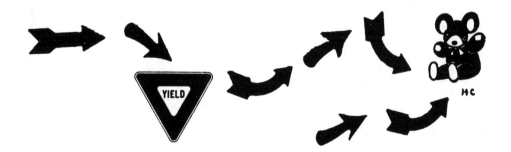

Mayflower

up ↑ 5

Obtain a large squash shaped roughly like a ship.

Using a picture of the Mayflower, put on sails, using thin wooden dowels for masts and paper for sails.

A TEACHER does not lay hands on a child's creation. She will not "show how" or "touch up" so parents will think the child's product credible.

SEQUENCE FOUR

DECEMBER

DECEMBER THEMES

Spool

Pine Cone

Pipe Cleaners

DECEMBER

Parties, Posadas and Paper Bag Reindeer

The December holidays bring *families and friends* together for fun, *feasting and gift-giving*. Greeting cards, photos, phone calls and visits draw aunts, uncles, cousins and grandparents close to us. Packages in bright wraps and trims appear like magic. Families celebrate special events during *Hanukkah, Christmas* (or *La Navidad*) and *Kwanza* festivities—each with its own cultural themes, foods, colors, songs and games. Homes are decorated with arts and crafts which reflect each family's ethnic and national origins.

Streets, shops and homes display *stars*, lights, candles, *gold and silver* trims, mythical creatures—so much to wonder about! However, Santa Claus, elves, Rudolph and other such friends are not stressed at a child care center. Children can share these friends and ideas with their families, at home, as each custom dictates.

Winter weather, in many areas of the United States, brings with it the need to bundle up. Hats, jackets, snow pants, mittens, boots—new challenges! Children need to practice *dressing skills* again! They are *patiently* taught to tie, button, zip and match up velcro *closers*.

We encourage children to decide when it is too cold to go outside, guided by *their* observations of the *thermometer* as it shows the *temperature*.

Clocks and *magnets* can be used to teach many concepts—*late/early*, half-an-hour, "just a minute," negative and positive.

Camels and *donkeys* often appear in holiday scenes. Some children have seen real ones; most, in America, have not. What are they? We can teach how these animals, common in Mexico, South and Central America and the Middle East, are a vital source of transport, much like trucks are on our highways.

Children can make and enjoy *traditional holiday foods* which come from many cultures. Potato Latkes with apple sauce; baked apples and cream (are you surprised to learn this is a Turkish dish?); dates and figs and pastries seasoned with spice. All cultures share a basic taste for butter and sugar pastries, from "Nana's" star-shaped Christmas cookies to loukoumades—deep fried and served with honey by "Yia Yia," a Greek grandmother. Rice dishes garnished with bright red pomegranate, yellow saffron or pignolas reflect Iranian, Egyptian and Indian heritages. Though our foods come from kitchens as far apart as Mexico and Iran, New England country kitchens or a Bedouin tent, still, each brings a common theme to our tables—*sharing a meal with others*. Some families sit on straw mats and eat fresh fruits at Kwanza, others sit around a *menorah* for the feasts of Hanukkah. All are thankful for blessings and remember loved ones as they share their foods.

Toys, spinning tops, dolls, children marching in a *posada*, garlands decorating trees, piñatas, stars—each suggests ways to explore motions, drama, music and stories.

The possibilities to extend language skills, to learn greetings in many languages, are especially rich during December.

JUST FOR FUN, how many words do your children know for "Peace"?

SEQUENCE FOUR

PEOPLE

up
↑
4

Uncles, Aunts and Cousins

Develop an understanding of the relationship to the child of uncles, aunts and cousins.

Ask: "How may uncles/aunts do you have? Which ones are your mother's brothers? Your father's brothers? Do they have any children? Are those children your brothers and sisters? Are they your grandparents? What are they then? Yes, they are cousins. How many cousins do you have altogether?"

6
↑
4

Letter Carriers

Explain that letter carriers are the people who bring mail to houses. They work for the United States Postal Service and they often wear uniforms. Usually they carry the letters in a leather sack but sometimes they push a little cart instead.

In the country, people often have mailboxes by the road, and the letter carrier delivers the mail from a car or truck.

How do they find the right letters to leave at each door or mailbox?

Set up a mail "route" in the room. Station the children along the route, giving them consecutive numbers. Put an envelope addressed to each child, with name and number, in a paper bag, all mixed together. Give the bag to the child chosen to be Letter Carrier, who takes out one letter at a time and delivers it. Time this.

Ask: What if the houses were scattered all over town? Would there be a faster way to do this?

Sort the letters and put them in order by number. Let the child deliver them again. Compare the times.

Note: A working letter carrier has a schedule to keep and can't take time to stop and talk to the children. Invite a *retired* letter carrier to come to the center to tell about the job.

EXPANDING OUR WORLD

5
↑
3

Post Office

Call the local Post Office and arrange a time when the children can visit. Usually it will be the Postmaster who will take them behind the scenes, show them how the mail is sorted, and explain what happens after it leaves there.

Holidays

We believe that children can expand their world when we expose them to the ways people of many cultures celebrate the mid-winter holiday, whether it be Hanukkah, Kwanza, Christmas or other. Santa Claus, Rudolph, and Christmas trees are there—on TV, in stores, on the street. We need to explain to parents our reasons for not stressing them at the center and enlist their cooperation in sharing their own traditional activities.

---

up
↑
3

Kwanza—What is it? (Afro-American, Multi-cultural)

Kwanza, which means "First Fruits," is an African holiday which has been adopted by some Afro-Americans. The celebration lasts from December 25 through December 31 and in many homes takes the place of the Christmas holiday.

The time is used to celebrate the good fortune which has come by hard work at school and in jobs. Presents are all handmade, as they were in centuries past.

The heart of Kwanza is the "Nguzo Saba," or the seven principles of life, which are:

1. Unoja—Unity
2. Kujichagulia—Self determination
3. Ujima—Collective work and responsibility
4. Ujamaa—Cooperative economics
5. Nia—Purpose
6. Kuumba—Creativity
7. Imani—Faith

- Show children Africa on a world map.

- Discuss the term Afro-Americans as people whose present families or ancestors came from Africa.

up ↑ 3 *Kwanza Celebration (Multi-cultural)*

The first thing necessary is a Kwanza table. Mats placed on the floor serve just as well. What goes on the table is as follows:

A straw mat which symbolizes the base of the family or household.

A straw basket in which tropical fruits are placed, symbolizing the fruits of the past year's hard work.

Dried ears of corn—an ear of corn for each member of the family (or each person present at the center).

Seven candles—Red, black and green candles, one to be lit each day when the family comes together to discuss the principle of the day.

A communal cup which is filled with wine (apple cider or fruit juice would do) and shared at meals.

The meal is eaten without utensils, using the right hand (finger foods).

If you have Afro-Americans in your center, plan a brief time each day to light another candle and talk about the principle for that day in terms the children can understand, eg. Unity—planning together at meeting time.

up ↑ 3 *Middle Eastern Peoples (Multi-cultural)*

Two major holidays which occur in December, Christmas and Hanukkah, have many cultural links to the countries of the Middle East.

- Show holiday cards with pictures of camels, shepherds, desert landscapes, palm trees; do not emphasize the religious aspect.

- Locate countries of the Middle East on a world map or globe. What do they have in common with Africa? (Both near equator, therefore hot climates.)

- Mention foods associated with the Middle East—dates, latkes, tabulleh.

Hanukkah Story (as told by Grace Mitchell)

up
↑
3

There was once a wicked king named Antiochus. He was a very proud king. "I am the greatest king of all," he said. "When my people walk near me they will bow down before me." The people did bow to Antiochus for they were afraid of him and his cruel punishments. He had many soldiers. The soldiers marched from town to town to see that the people obeyed the harsh laws of Antiochus and bowed before him and his statues.

In a village called Modin, there lived a man named Mattathias. He had five sons, Judah, Jonathan, Jochanon, Simon and Eleazar. (Suggest counting with fingers.) Mattathias and his sons were Jews and they believed only in God. They prayed to Him in their temples. They refused to bow to Antiochus. They were not afraid of him.

Antiochus was very angry when he heard of this. He ordered his soldiers to go to the village and fight Mattathias and his sons. Many of the villagers heard that Antiochus' soldiers were coming and they fled into the hills with Mattathias and his sons to form an army. This little army hid in the caves on the hills. They chose Judah, the eldest son, as their leader. He was called Judah Maccabee, Judah the Strong.

The army of Antiochus reached the village of Modin, and when they found none of Mattathias' men there, they broke into the temples and destroyed many of the beautiful things inside. They tore down the temples of Jerusalem, smashing the altar which was sacred to the Jews. When the army in the hills heard of this, they were outraged and they went into Modin to drive away Antiochus and his men. They fought bravely and defeated the army and drove them away from their lands.

The women of Modin cheered their brave men and welcomed them home from their successful battle. Together the villagers cleaned and restored the temple and refilled the oil lamps which were always left burning in honor of their God. But they discovered that the oil for the lamps had been spilled by the soldiers and that there was so little it would only burn for one day. They sent a messenger to run through the hills and into another village for more of the precious oil. It was a long, hard journey and would take at least eight days. The Jews in Modin waited patiently, watching the flickering lamps, knowing that they could not burn until the messenger came with more oil. While they waited, they made food for the tired army, a special food called latkes, pancakes made from potatoes.

To the amazement of the villagers, the little lamps continued to burn. One day passed, two days, three—still the lamps burned. By now, the messenger was through the mountains and crossing the wide valley below. On the fourth day, he reached the village where he bought the new oil. It would take four days to return to Modin.

When he returned he was surprised to find the lamps of the temple still burning. God must have made the lamps burn on. The villagers celebrated, saying this was a miracle of God. They danced, sang and offered feasts in honor of their God for the miracle of lights, Hanukkah.

During this festival of lights, the Jews have many special celebrations. They make latkes and eat them with applesauce or sour cream. The children are given special Hanukkah gifts and money which they call gelt. They play games with a dreidel, a spinning top made for Hanukkah.

Hanukkah days are happy days, days for joining with family and friends in gift giving and feasting, days for remembering the happy miracle of the lights—Hanukkah.

Christmas Story (as told by Grace Mitchell)

up
↑
3

There was once a king whose name was Herod. He ruled in a land called Judea, near where Israel and Palestine are today. Herod was a very severe and strict king. He made a law that all of the people of his country had to go to the villages where their parents and grandparents had been born and write their names in a big, black book, called a census book. This was because Herod wanted to charge every person a tax to live in Judea. He would punish anyone who did not go to be counted and pay the tax.

Many of the people lived far away from the places where they had been born. In those days, there were no cars, planes or trains to travel from place to place. The roadways were rough and it took many days of hard walking to reach the towns where the people were counted and paid their taxes.

There were two travelers whose names were Mary and Joseph. They had a long way to travel. They had a donkey; he was little but his back was strong and he carried Mary all the way. Mary was soon going to have a baby and Joseph walked beside her, guiding the little donkey over the rough and narrow pathways. After many days they came to Bethlehem, the town where Joseph's grandfather had lived. They were very tired and they were hungry. Mary needed food and rest. It was near the time when her baby would be born.

Joseph comforted her and said, "I will find you some warm food and a comfortable bed in an inn." But Joseph did not realize how many others had come to Bethlehem to be counted. The inns were crowded; there were no more rooms. Joseph and Mary went from one to another asking for a place to rest but each time Joseph knocked at the door, the busy innkeepers would snap at him rudely saying, "No room! No room!" Some even slammed their doors. (It was a busy time for them and they had forgotten their manners.)

Finally, Joseph and Mary came to the very last inn at Bethlehem. It, too, was filled. Poor Joseph begged, "Please, I must find a place for my wife, Mary, to rest, for her baby will soon be born."

The innkeeper's wife stood nearby and heard his pleading. She looked at Mary and felt sorry for her. "You could go into our stable." she said. "It will be warm and there is fresh hay to make into a bed. I will bring you some food."

Joseph and Mary were grateful for this kind woman's offer. They went into the stable and found it warmed by the heat from the animals' bodies. There was a cow, an ox, some sheep and goats and Joseph's own little donkey. They fixed a bed in the manger with sweet, fresh hay. Late that night, just when the animals had fallen asleep, they were roused by the tiny cry of a newborn baby. A baby boy was born to Mary and Joseph. Mary wrapped him snugly in clean cloth and laid him in the crib. She named him Jesus.

Later, some wise men and shepherds from far away came to bring gifts to the new baby. They had been told that Jesus would be born and that he would grow to become a great king. They wanted to share in the celebration of his birth.

Jesus did grow up to become a very great man. He went as a teacher throughout the country and taught people how kindness and love toward all mankind would bring happiness and peace to the world. This happened a long time ago, nearly two thousand years ago. Still, people remember the lessons of Jesus and each year on December 25th, Jesus' birthday, some gather to celebrate the event.

Christmas is a happy time when people share gifts, songs and special foods. It is a time to remember those we love and to practice sharing and kindness.

Among the special symbols of Christmas, which you will see as people begin to decorate for their celebrations, is the star. This is the sign of Christmas because on the night Jesus was born, a very bright star shone in the skies over Bethlehem.

December

up ↑ 3 | *La Navidad (Mexico, Hispanics)*

Tell the children: In Mexico, Christmas (Navidad) begins December 16th. Each evening for nine days, groups of children and adults take part in the *posada*. The word *posada* means "inn" or "place of lodging," and the people go in a procession (parade) to a different home each night. They often dress in costumes and carry lighted candles, and usually two of the children carry a small platform on which are figures of Mary (on a donkey) and Joseph.

Children knock on the door and are told "There is no room," but after they have turned away, they are invited in for a party. On the last night, December 24, they are invited in right away. As they leave, you will hear them calling out "Feliz Navidad" (Fay-LEES Nah-vee-DAHD)—in other words, "Merry Christmas."

SKILLS FOR DAILY LIVING

5 ↑ 2 | *Dressing (Outside Clothing) (Routines)*

Toddlers: when they recognize their own jackets, teach them to bring to adults for help.

When children are able to spread jackets on floor, inside facing up, teach them to lie, back on jacket, head above collar, and slip arms into sleeves.

Children next learn to slip arms into sleeves when someone else is holding jacket. Finally, they can hold jackets themselves, putting arms into first one sleeve, then the other.

Another technique which fairly young children (3) can learn goes as follows: child spreads jacket on the floor and stands at collar, leans over and puts arms into sleeves, then flips the jacket over head, at the same time standing up. (See poem "Jacket Flip" below.)

Boots should be kept with jacket and clipped with spring clothespin. It will save time to put children's names in boots and mark LEFT and RIGHT with magic marker.

Mittens, if dry, should be put in jacket pockets; if wet, clipped together and hung over a line.

up ↑ 3 | *Jacket Flip*

> To help get dressed for out-of-door
> Lay your coat flat on the floor
> Back side down your jacket goes,
> Then, stand with collar at your toes.
> Push both hands into the sleeves
> Till fingers peek out, if you please.
> Hold the cuffs in a strong grip
> Then over your head the jacket flip!
> Pull it tight across your chest
> Then zip or button—you're all dressed.

5 ↑ 2 | *Garment Fasteners (Routines)*

Buttons, zippers, ties, "Velcro," take *lots* of practice. Provide toys which use these skills.

Fasten a jacket around the back of a chair and let child open and close front.

4 ↑ 2 | *Hat Rack*

Attach gallon plastic jugs, using dowels, to a board. Add faces with various expressions. Make up games using the Hat Rack. Use hats with snaps, velcro or ties to practice skills.

- Put blue hat on happy face.
- Pull stocking cap on sad face.
- Which one is the baker's hat? Put it on the angry face.
- Put only the winter hats on the heads.
- Which hats are for rainy weather?

Note: Children should not swap hats for hygienic reasons.

up ↑ 4 | *Climate Clothing*

Mount on cards pictures of clothing suitable for various climates and weather conditions. Make a chart or sorting boxes marked with symbols to represent weather conditions.

Ask children to sort clothing into appropriate categories.

Ethan is traveling to Florida (hot place). What should he pack to wear?

Tomorrow it may snow. Find three clothing items we will need to wear outside.

Show a map of the United States with colored climate divisions. Explain the cold, warm, hot areas. Determine appropriate clothing for each area.

Look at pictures of people wearing various kinds of clothing. Ask: "What is the weather like where these people are?"

up ↑ 3 | *Clothing Thermometer*

Teach children how to read an outside thermometer. Put a clothing gauge on the inside wall/window casing near the thermometer which shows pictures of clothing appropriate to current temperature.

Attach an arrow to point to the pictures.

CONCEPTS

5 ↑ 3 | *Loud/Soft*

Teacher explains that when everybody shouts, our voices are *loud* and we say it is *noisy*, but when we whisper, our voices are *soft* and the room is *quiet*.

Say: "Some animals make *loud* noises, some are *soft*. Tell me which kind of a noise this animal makes." (Hold up pictures of cow, cat, dog, lion, mouse, rooster, chicken.) Let the children make the noise and decide whether it is loud or soft.

December

Gold/Silver
- Show assorted objects of gold/silver colors. Ask children to sort into each color.
- Children hunt for gold and silver in the room. (Tip: plan to wear some gold or silver jewelry that day.)
- Provide gold and silver stars to stick onto black or blue paper.

Triangles to Stars
Give an assortment of triangular shaped papers and ask children to put them together to form stars. Paste on a sheet of paper. Outline the outer edges to show the star shape.

Triangle Hunt
- Cut triangles of various angles and sizes from cardboard. Match with objects, inside and outside—gables, traffic signs, pavement patterns, tree limb patterns, etc.
- Fold in the corners of square/rectangular papers. Unfold and draw lines along all the folds, creating triangles. Color the triangles, using several different colors.

Star Search
- Put star shapes and pictures of stars (greeting cards) around the room. Children search, gather and count stars.
- SCHOOL AGE children count the stars they see but do not gather.
- SCHOOL AGE use a timer and set a 5-minute limit for the search.

SCIENCE

Multi-cultural Foods for Holidays

The major holidays which occur in December suggest special foods. Different ethnic groups bring their particular dishes to these holidays. In America, the variations seem endless as each group adapts its heritage to new ingredients and cooking methods.

Look around you. How many cultures could add their "traditional" dishes to your holiday observances? Invite parents and staff to share their recipes and, when possible, come and cook with the children. (Note: Keep in mind local health regulations which may prohibit serving food at child care centers which is not cooked on the premises.)

Avoid special holiday foods requiring long and complicated preparation and minimal participation by children. Encourage simple, child-oriented, hands-on cooking.

Latkes (Hanukkah, Multi-cultural, Middle East)
Ingredients:

4 very large potatoes	1/2 tsp salt
2 eggs	1/2 tsp baking powder
4 tbsp grated onion	2 tbsp cracker crumbs or Matzo meal

Peel and grind potatoes. Drain off liquid. Beat eggs and stir into potato. Grate onion, measure, stir into potato, along with salt and baking powder and crumbs.

Drop by teaspoons onto frying pan with about 1/2 inch very hot fat. Fry and turn pancakes until brown. Drain on paper towels.

Serve warm with apple sauce, sour cream or yogurt.

Keep children well back while frying as hot fat may spatter.

Spice Test

up ↑ 3

Many of our familiar spices come from the Middle East.

Put samples of cinnamon, nutmeg, ginger into small containers (margarine tubs) and stretch fabric over the top. Identify by the smells.

Sprinkle a *little* of each mixed with sugar onto toast samples. Taste test.

Serve cinnamon grahams; ginger cookies; nutmeg flavored pastry. Ask children to identify by spice used.

Karamu/Kwanza Feast (Afro-Americans/Multi-cultural)

up ↑ 3

Decorate place mats and table with black, red and green. Serve fresh fruits and raw (or slightly cooked for TODDLERS) vegetables with yogurt and cheese dips. Try with sprinkles of spices (see above).

Ask children which are fruits and which are vegetables. TODDLERS practice eating skills using small plastic forks to spear foods.

As children feast, ask: "What are some good things to do for other people?" Talk about such ideas as sharing food and toys (good deeds) and setting and cleaning the table together (community services).

Stuffed Dates

up ↑ 2

Cut open dates lengthwise with a plastic knife. Remove pits.

Using small knives, children fill with peanut butter, then roll in granulated sugar.

Variations: Fill with cream cheese and pineapple or plain cream cheese, then dip into crushed peanuts.

Show pictures of date palms and tell children where dates can be grown.

Camels and Donkeys

up ↑ 5

Display pictures. Talk about the likenesses/differences. Ask: What do camels (donkeys) do? How do they work for people? How are they like horses?

Show these animals carrying burdens (National Geographic Magazine). Explain why camels are suited to the desert. (Wide flat feet to walk on sand, hump/s to store food, can go a long time with very little water.)

In Middle East, Africa and Latin American countries, these "beasts of burden" are still a common method of freight and transport. Show large trailer trucks which transport foods and other freight. Compare differences. Ask How do trucks run? (Gasoline, diesel) How do animals "run"? (Grazing, grains)

Potatoes and Yams

up ↑ 4

- Plant potato "eye" in soil in a glass jar.
- Use three toothpicks stuck in the side to suspend a yam on a glass with half of the yam under water.
- Watch the two kinds of potatoes as they grow. Note likenesses and differences in color, shape and size of leaves.

  Transplant outside when weather is suitable. Dig up in early summer to see the tiny potatoes. These "seed" potatoes can also be replanted.

Charcoal

December

up ↑ 5

Evergreens

Lay out branch samples ("leaves") from several types of evergreens—pine, spruce, hemlock, juniper, arbor vitae. Discuss the likenesses and differences. Count needles in each bunch—pines vary, each species can be identified by the needle type. Smell. Why are they called "evergreens"?

Show pictures of trees, match to the samples. Look for real trees which match the samples and also the pictures.

5 ↑ 3

Clock Numbers

- In preparation for clock study, make a set of sturdy cards with numbers one through twelve. Use in sequence and counting activities.

- Children arrange scattered numbers in numerical order

- Arrange cards in numerical order, have one child leave the room. Remove one number. The child returns, observes numbers, and guesses which number was removed.

up ↑ 4

Clock on the Floor

- Make a large circle in chalk on floor. Place plastic or cardboard numbers indicating hours on a clock face and large cardboard pointers to use as clock hands. One child "sets hands" by moving pointers to two numbers.

- Set hands of clock. Children march around the circle to music. When the music stops, the children who are at the numbers designated by clock hands call them out. The next step in difficulty is to name the time shown.

- Remove hands. Children stand around outside of circle, each at a number. Call out names of two children and put hands back, pointing to the children named. Others say what time is shown.

- Make a set of cards with symbols representing activities throughout the day such as:

  car—driving to childcare; a glass and a cracker—snack time; a swing set—playground time; a place setting—lunch time; a cot—nap time; paintbrush & paints—painting or activity time.

  One child lies on the floor inside circle, using arms to represent clock hands. Other children take turns drawing cards and calling them out. Child on floor "sets the clock" to the right time for the activity shown on the card.

up ↑ 3 **Sand Clock (Timer)**

Demonstrate a three minute egg timer. Play games, relay races; time actions using the timer. Some suggestions:

- How many times can you walk around the table before the sand runs out?

- Can you do the puzzle in three minutes?

- Cook three minute eggs. How many turns of the timer are necessary for hard-boiled eggs?

- Use the timer to prepare children for changes, i.e. "When the sand runs through, we will stop and put the blocks away."

up ↑ 5 **Minutes (School Age)**

Mark off 1-60 on a circle to represent minutes in an hour. Divide circle into half and quarter segments to demonstrate half and quarter hours; or fold a paper circle into half and quarter sections to show segments of hours.

5 ↑ 3 **Demagnetization**

U-shaped magnets will lose their magnetic properties if they are stored with like poles (positive/negative) facing in the same direction. They should be stored in a single layer in alternate positions. Teach this to the children by marking storage boxes with the magnet shapes as they should be stored.

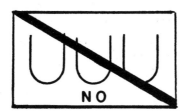
NO

YES

5 ↑ 3 **Magnets**

Provide assorted objects both magnetic and non-magnetic for child to sort using magnets. Ask child to place magnetic (Yes) objects in a green container and non-magnetic (No) objects in a red container.

up ↑ 3 **Magnetic Fish**

Cut fish shapes from plastic (coffee can lids). Slip a paper clip onto the "mouth" end. Attach small magnets to fishing lines and use to catch fish from tubs.

Cardboard/paper fish can be fished out of "dry" ponds as well.

Vary the activity by marking fish with numbers, letters, shapes, concepts, colors. Captured fish are sorted into sets by size, color, etc.

5 ↑ 3 **Magnetic Balloons**

Inflate balloons and rub with a wool cloth or against woolen clothing. The static electricity will cause the balloons to cling or stick to things.

Put several magnetized balloons into a large carton. They will jump away (repel) each other.

Try putting two magnets with like poles together. An invisible force pushes them apart.

December

5↑3 ***Magnet Games (Sets, Sequences, Spatial)***
Use novelty magnets on a metal tray (fruits, vegetables, shapes, animals, flowers, etc.) in sorting, matching, concept games. Give directions:

- Put three flower magnets in a row.

- Put the apples *under* the banana; put the grape *beside* the apples; put three pears *around* the apple.

Teacher lays a group of magnets across the top of the tray. Child copies the arrangement with matching magnets.

- Put all the animals on the *left* side. Put all the flower magnets on the *right* side.

up↑4 ***Magnetic Letters/Numbers (Reading Readiness)***
Use cookie sheets (non-aluminum) as playboards for magnetic letters and numbers. Attach a long pocket along the top edge of the tray to hold paper strips on which various words, letter and numeral sets/combinations, phone numbers, names, etc. can be printed.

Child arranges magnets in matching combinations.

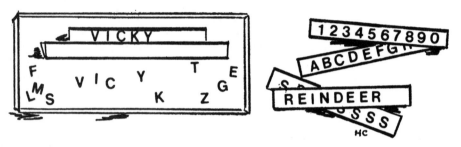

5↑3 ***Magnetic Window***
Collect iron filings from a machine shop/welder/plumber (about one cup). Tape inside two pieces of clear plastic (about 12" square). Keep the plastic apart, *slightly*, by putting a strip of thin cardboard/oak tag around the inner edges.

Children draw magnets over the plastic attracting the filings into designs and clusters.

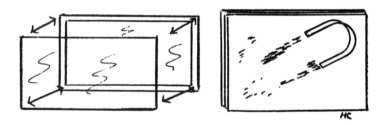

MUSIC—MOVEMENT

5↑3 ***Top Spin***
Mark circles or lay hoops on the floor. Children spin around inside circles. Use a music box to time the spins. If "tops" touch, they must sit in their circle.

Give each child a scarf or streamer to flutter while spinning.

5 ↑ 3 *Toy Match-Up*

- Substitute the name of a toy for "Lassie" in the song "Did You Ever See a Lassie?". Put a collection of toys (various objects) behind a screen or in a large carton. Children take turns finding the toy used in the song.

- Give each child a picture of a toy. Children show pictures in turn; group sings while child finds toy matching the picture.

- Lay pictures out. Children choose and find toy matches.

5 ↑ 3 *Toys in Motion*

The teacher plays a music box (if possible, one that has a moving doll). Ask children to talk about different toys and move like each one, to be wooden soldiers, dancing dolls, rag dolls, drums, trumpets, balls, puppets on string, wind up cars. The "toymaker" winds up each toy and the rest guess what toy it is.

5 ↑ 3 *Star Sort ("Twinkle, Twinkle, Little Star")*

- Lay out four to ten stars of graduated sizes—tiny to large. One child rearranges by size while others sing the song, one verse for each turn. As children become more adept, add more sizes and/or sing the song at a faster tempo.

- Children sit in a circle. Stars of various sizes are placed behind each child. One child is chosen to walk around the outside to choose a star. Others sing the song, with variations: "Twinkle, twinkle tiny (great big, smallest, etc.) star."

2 ↑ 1 *Baby-Toddler Exercise Course*

Use large cartons and tubes to create a "creeping-and-crawling" course for the babes and toddlers who spend most of their time on the floor. Secure the crawl-throughs as necessary with tape and props. Use various textures (rugs, linoleum scraps, cloth, fake fur) on the "paths" between the units. Hang paper, plastic and/or cloth fringes across the openings. Put various textures, pictures and mirrors (securely taped at edges) on inner and outer walls.

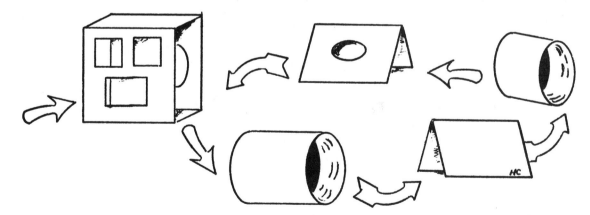

3 ↑ 2 *Box Path-Ladder Course*

Attach shoe boxes to long strips of cardboard (or wide wooden boards). Lay together to create a "step-in" walk. Use the covers for lower "step-ins." Add a ladder for older children. Include rope "handrails" attached to wall if needed or, for a more portable walk, set up the box strips between a row of chairs with the backs used as handrails.

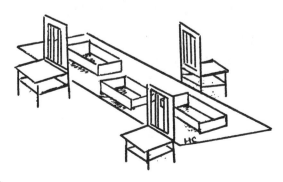

LANGUAGE—DRAMA

Addresses

- Ask: What is your address? Practice saying town, street and house number. Some 5's can write the information. Make a chart listing names of the children. Fill in spaces beside the name as children are able to name the parts of their addresses.

- Ask parents to supply addressed envelopes showing the child's address. Put beside the name on the chart and also at the child's cubby.

- Ask parents to put a stamp inside an addressed envelope for their child to bring. Child dictates a message and makes a card to enclose and send home.

Write a Letter

Teacher, write a letter to your class and mail it, and when it arrives, talk about where you wrote it, where it has been, who brought it to the school. Help the children write a letter to someone (mayor, prominent community person). (The teacher should enclose a personal note explaining the project and requesting a response.) Address, stamp and mail the letter; if possible, walk to a nearby post office or box.

Postcards

- Ask parents and other relatives to send postcards when they go on trips. Make into scrapbooks with a sentence for each card—"John's father sent it from Florida." "Kate's grandmother sent it from London."

- File the postcards by location in a box.

- Post a map of the world or the U.S. Put the postcards up around the map. Stretch yarn lines from the postcards to the places they represent on the map.

Post Office Play (On-going)

Turn the housekeeping/dramatic play area into a Post Office. Have letter slots in a carton, a counter for selling stamps, a U.S. Post Office sign, mail bags, etc. Play with stamps which come in junk mail.

Children make and send cards to each other to be picked up at "General Delivery" or hand-delivered.

Presents/Ten Questions

- Children divide into two groups. Group one leaves the room. Teacher chooses one to be the "present." "Present" hides inside a box. Group two asks 10 (6,8) questions (yes/no responses) to determine identity of "present."

- Group one chooses an object as the present and group two guesses.

Dreidel Games (Multi-cultural, Hanukkah)

- Spin dreidels and use in games to teach various concepts by changing symbols, using words such as up/down/over/under/soft/loud. Children take turns spinning dreidel and acting out the concept.

- Play "Put and Take" games—dreidel symbols read "put two," "take one," etc. Children use play money (gelt) or tokens. Each player is given (6,8,10) tokens depending on number playing. Children give and take tokens according to the symbol showing when top spins and falls to one side.

To make dreidels, push pencils (pointed dowels) through 1/2 pint milk cartons, boxes or drilled blocks. Put a thread spool inside a small box and glue a dowel or pencil into the hole.

- Paste shapes, objects, colors, letters, numerals, etc. to the dreidel sides. Children find, match, make the objects shown.
- Paste faces displaying emotions to sides. Children mime faces.

CREATIVE PROJECTS

Piñatas

up ↑ 3

This favorite Mexican holiday treat may be constructed in the following ways:

- Puff out paper bags. Stuff with tissue to hold shape desired. Cover with strips of starched tissue. Remove stuffing when dry. Decorate.
- Blow up balloons and cover with mâchè.
- Make duplicate shapes, such as stars, birds, animals, etc. from large pieces of tissue (three or four thicknesses), painted newsprint or wrapping paper. Staple the two shapes together at edges and stuff with shreds of paper to hold out shape. Cover this with starched wet paper and allow to dry. When dry, remove stuffing.

Fill piñatas with wrapped candies or other small treats. Decorate cardboard tube to use as striker for breaking open piñata. (Read *Nine Days to Christmas* by Marie Hall Ets (pub. Viking).)

Menorah

up ↑ 4

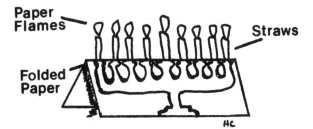

Star Prints

5 ↑ 3

Use cookie cutters and various printing materials cut in the shape of stars. Dip into tempera paint and print stars on paper, cloth, card folders and other art projects.

up ↑ 4
Triangle Trees
Cut triangle shapes from green paper, magazine pictures (green parts) or cloth and paste onto a large mural to create an evergreen forest effect or use the shapes to fill a large triangular shaped tree.

up ↑ 3
Garlands/Chains (Patterns, Sequences)
- Make garlands and chains using various materials: paper, rings, macaroni, tube sections, cranberries, beads. Use the activity to create color and shape patterns, i.e. red, green, black, etc; curved (macaroni), straight, curly, etc.

- Older children may copy specific patterns (2, 3, 2, 3, 2, 3) with different items.

- Garlands, paper chains, etc. can be on-going projects. Measure garlands every week, record length. Lay out in designs, paths to follow, shapes. How many times will garland go around a room, table, etc.?

4 ↑ 2
Tubes/Cans (Toddlers, Too!)
Paper tubes cut into 2"-3" sections and small size cardboard juice cans can be strung by TODDLERS on short (2'-3') sections of clothesline with a cardboard "stopper" knotted onto one end to prevent tubes from slipping off.

Paint tubes with colors. Ask child to string "a red (other colors) ring" or "put two green rings on the rope," etc. Or: string a second garland side-by-side with a toddler. Ask the child to choose the same color you have and/or follow the child's lead and copy that pattern.

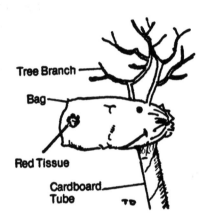

Tree Branch

Bag

Red Tissue

Cardboard Tube

up ↑ 5
Reindeer
Stuff a paper bag with newspaper. Insert two bare tree branches. Secure with masking tape. Insert a long paper tube into bag and secure with tape. Add eyes, nose, mouth.

JUST FOR FUN

up ↑ 2
Posada Party
Over a period of a week, prepare for a Posada Party. (See La Navidad)
- Improvise costumes.

- Make cardboard "candles" with yellow paper "flames."

- Make a piñata.

- Learn to say *Feliz Navidad.* (Fay-LEES Nah-vee-DAHD)

- Make a platform and find small figures to represent Mary, Joseph and the donkey.

- On the day of the party, the children march around in a procession, going "door-to-door" (activity centers). Teachers are hosts. Some lead a song, some play a game, at one the children break a piñata. Last host serves a treat.

SEQUENCE FIVE

JANUARY

JANUARY THEMES

JANUARY

Popcorn and Paper Snowballs

Everyone is **alike**—people share many common attributes—families, foods, work and homes. They enjoy music, games, toys, sweets! People everywhere cope with **climate** and wear special clothes for very **hot** or very **cold** weather.

Everyone is **different**. Each culture, country and climate produces special characteristics—foods, clothes, homes, and language which set groups of people apart. How are **Alaskans (Eskimos)** and **Hispanic Americans** alike? How are they **different**? Identical **twins** look alike. How are they different?

The **climate**, **homes**, **food**, clothing and lifestyles of people differ greatly between such **hot places** as **Hawaii** and **cold places** like **Alaska**. In mid-winter, some people surf in **California** while others toboggan in Maine. Yarn lines stretched between places on postcards to their spots on a globe or map might be a child's first "geography" lesson.

Snow and **ice**; warm, insulated parkas are a part of the scene in Wisconsin—in contrast to beach umbrellas, lounge chairs and swimsuits in Florida.

Wherever people live—suburban subdivisions, apartments, condominiums, high rises, trailers, tents, hogans—if they are **physically challenged** (NOT "handicapped"), they need special help such as ramps, **Braille**, reserved spaces, hearing aids, special bathrooms and door openers.

All **snowflakes** are **hexagons** and **white**. White comes in many shades, just as do red or blue or green. When is **hot**, hot or **cold**, cold? Where do animals live and what are their **homes** called?

January science activities also explore **freezing** and **melting water**. Children learn how we **measure temperature** with **thermometers**; days with **calendars**; liquid and dry materials with **cups**, **gallons**, **teaspoons**, etc.

Activities explore the senses of **touch** with Braille games, touch trails, and feely boxes. Children identify textures and objects through touching.

BIG words—"experiment," "identify," "thermometer"—and little words—"No Blocks Today"—are explored, not because we expect young children to "read," but because using all kinds of words in conversation and on signs is part of **reading readiness**. When children are learning to read they need to be able to distinguish between "b" and "d," "m" and "w," "3" and "8." Signs posted at activity centers help to teach children that symbols (letters and numerals) are used to make **words**. Words are put together in **sentences** to make **stories**. Some words **rhyme**—they sound **alike**.

Whether lounges, swivelers or rockers, **chairs** can be used to explore all kinds of motions. Ice, toboggans, skates, snow—each one is a theme to develop through motions and sounds.

Children make scrapbook houses and popcorn macaroons, go "ice fishing," toss paper snowballs and explore **POPCORN**—JUST FOR FUN!

January

SEQUENCE FIVE

PEOPLE

up ↑ 4 | *Office Workers*

Put out an assortment (items/pictures) of office tools and equipment such as stapler, punch, rulers, tape, pictures of various machines. Ask who uses and how various things are used? Where are offices in the center?

Visit and find some of the same items.

Parents of the children at the center who work in offices might come and tell about three or four tasks they perform at offices and show items/tools they use.

up ↑ 4 | *Likenesses and Differences*

*   Sit in a circle. Each child looks at the person beside him/her and names physical features which are alike and others which are different:

    "Kerry and I both have (blue eyes, long hair, etc.)."

    "I have black curly hair, Kerry has straight braids."

*   How is everyone alike? (Two eyes, ears, teeth, etc.)

*   In what ways are we different? (Age, height, skin color, etc.)

*   Why is it good that we are not all just alike?

up ↑ 3 | *Twins*

Discuss identical twins with the children. Show pictures and tell stories about them. Invite real twins to come and visit.

EXPANDING OUR WORLD

> **PEOPLE WHO ARE PHYSICALLY CHALLENGED**
>
> Whether or not you have any physically challenged children (or staff) at the center, all children will come in contact with such people in the course of their lives. Help them to understand that the external *differences* are not as important as internal *likenesses*.

up ↑ 3 | *Challenges—Helping to Meet Them*

Take a field trip to a building where you can see:

*   Braille markers (elevators)

    Show children the Braille markers in elevators and other public places. Feel the shapes of the numbers. Can the children find a specific floor number with eyes closed?

*   Ramps, accessible bathrooms, and reserved parking spaces

*   Visit a bathroom equipped for people using wheelchairs. How is it different? Why?

*   Show the symbols used to indicate accessible features in buildings and on streets, parking places, sidewalks.

*   Why do we need ramps? Back at the center, build ramps with blocks. Use toy cars to demonstrate the needs of people in wheelchairs.

Living Places and Spaces

- Ask: What kinds of homes do people live in? List the ideas.

- Make a picture collage showing houses, cottages, huts, cabins, castles, palaces, apartments, mansions, duplex, motel, hotel, trailer, dormitory, prison, houseboat, tent, teepee, wigwam, hogan, igloo, etc.

- How many different kinds of houses do the people in the classroom live in? What are the materials used to make houses?

- Put pictures of a farm, jungle, ocean and house across a large piece of cardboard. Under each one make a pocket. Children cut/draw pictures of people, fish, animals, etc. Mount on construction paper and sort into pockets. Older children might also add word labels to pictures.

Homes of Children

A child's home provides the crucial elements for healthy growth. How and where do I live? Where do I sleep, eat, play? How are the different rooms or sections of my house used? What things belong to me? What things are used by the whole family?

Put out an assortment of household items. Ask children to sort into uses and/or places used—kitchen, bath, bedroom, playroom, living room.

At first, children may think of just their own rooms, toys and belongings. Then they begin to understand what belongs to the entire family. At the center, children can be encouraged to describe their homes and families in order to develop a sense of pride and place in their homes.

Climate Differences

Discuss differences in climate and how climate affects people. What people live in cold places? Hot places? What do they wear? What kinds of houses do they live in?

Make a display of various kinds of homes or use magazine pictures to illustrate variety of homes.

Show equator on a globe. Tell children it is the hottest part of the world. (Do not try to explain why.) See what countries are close to the equator.

Latin America/Spain (Hispanics) (Multi-cultural)

- Explore these places using pictures, stories, songs, and foods. Ask people from these cultures to visit and share their lives with the children.

- Talk about what it is like to live in a warm to hot climate.

- Teach some Spanish words for things common to all people—house-casa, boy-niño, girl-niña, milk-leche.

Alaska/Canada (Eskimos) (Multi-cultural)

- Show Alaska and Canada on a globe. Point out how close they are to the North Pole and tell them the North and South Poles are the two coldest places in the world. (Do not try to explain why.) Show *winter* scenes of Alaska.

- Using pictures, compare:

snow and ice	to	jungle, rain forest
fur parkas	to	bathing suits
dog sleds	to	canoes
igloos*	to	thatched huts

*Explain that these were the early homes, seldom found today.

- With school age children, learn about tundra, glaciers, and words that have been adopted from the Eskimos: mukluk, parka, kayak.

SKILLS FOR DAILY LIVING

Table Clearing

After the noon meal, all children help to clear.

a. Teacher fills two pans or buckets with soapy water.

b. Children scrape food scraps into trash barrel.

c. Children put plates, cups into one pan, eating utensils into the other.

d. Each child uses napkins to wipe crumbs off table, then puts napkin in barrel.

e. Assigned children use damp sponge to clean off table and wipe up spills, then sweep around table.

Go through this process daily with the children, until they have all learned each routine.

Citrus Fruits (Vitamin C)

In winter, we need an extra supply of Vitamin C to stay healthy. Vitamin C is found in citrus fruits such as oranges, grapefruit, lemons, pineapple.

- Show pictures of these fruits, growing and in store displays.
- Serve orange slices, fresh pineapple chunks for snacks.
- Squeeze lemons with the children and make lemonade.

Sunglasses (Eskimos) (Multi-cultural)

Make sunglasses by cutting narrow slits in strips of cardboard. Tie string or elastic on ends. Wear outside in bright sunlight. Discuss how this helps protect their eyes against the glare of the sun on snow. The early Eskimos used such glasses.

CONCEPTS

5 ↑ 3 *Cold-Hot*

Ask children to name some cold things, then some hot things. List them on a chalkboard or easel.

- Make a collage of pictures to go with either cold or hot.

- Make books for either cold or hot, or a Hot-Cold book with pictures of cold things on one page and hot things on the facing page.

up ↑ 3 *White*

Show the differences in shades of white. Compare "white" clothing, show paint charts, paper, flowers, snow, dishes. SCHOOL AGE can learn some of the shade names—ivory, cream, bone, egg-shell, etc.

up ↑ 4 *Hexagon (Snowflakes)*

Show children a hexagon and tell them this is the basic six-sided shape of a snowflake. Show snowflake photographs in books (some dictionaries).

Give children a hexagon-shaped piece of white paper. Ask them to fold the paper and cut sections out. Unfold to reveal their snowflakes. Mount on dark paper or hang from ceiling.

SCIENCE

5 ↑ 3 *Popcorn*

Pop, eat, enjoy!

- Put some in a bag. Feel the outside of the bag. How does it feel? List the words used to describe the smell, taste, feel, look. Compare the *sounds* of popcorn.

- Shake the uncooked kernels in a bag, then the popped corn.

- How is popped corn alike/different from kernel or creamed corn and corn on the cob?

up ↑ 3 *Popcorn Macaroons (Coconut, Recipe)*

3 cups popped, unsalted popcorn	1/4 tsp salt
2 egg whites	1 tsp sugar
1/4 cup sugar	1/3 cup shredded coconut

Directions:

Whirl popcorn in blender, one cup at a time until you have 1 1/2 cups finely ground popcorn. Set aside.

In medium bowl beat egg whites to stiff peaks. Add sugar gradually at lower speed. Beat in vanilla. Gradually fold in the popcorn and coconut.

Drop by teaspoons onto oiled baking sheet. Bake 325° for 10 to 12 minutes until lightly browned.

Remove immediately from sheets and cool. (24 macaroons)

Coconut Oat Cookies (Recipe)

1 cup margarine	1/4 cup corn syrup
1 1/2 cup brown sugar	1 unbeaten egg
1 1/4 cup rolled oats	1 cup coconut
1 1/2 cup flour	1/4 tsp salt
1/2 tsp baking powder	

Cream margarine and sugar, add egg and syrup, beat. Mix in dry ingredients and drop by spoonfuls on greased cookie sheet, two inches apart. Bake in pre-heated oven at 350° from 8 to 10 minutes.

Homes for Animals and Birds

Show pictures of various animals and ask: Where (what kind of places) do these animals live?

Collect pictures of animal and bird dwellings—nest, den, coop, cage, cave, hole, hutch, barn, stable, shed, web, rookery, hive, lodge (beaver's). Does a fish have a house? What kinds of materials are used for animal homes?

Onion Sprouting

Put three toothpicks into large onion and suspend over a small glass of water, so that only the bottom is in the water. Place in a sunny window and watch for leaf sprouts. Replace water as needed. When roots form, transplant to a pot of rich soil.

Pineapple

Slice off top two inches of a pineapple, leaving green top attached; allow to dry for ten days. Plant it in damp, sandy soil. Keep moist. When roots begin to sprout (about one month), transplant it to a larger pot of sandy potting soil. For another, faster way, read *Growing Up Green*, by Skelsey and Huckaby (pub. Workman).

Sight (Observation)

Develop the children's powers of observation with the following activities:

- Children line up in two teams. Players in one team have their backs turned, the others each swap something in their wearing apparel. The first team then tries to guess what change was made. (SCHOOL AGE)

- Children wear mittens of various colors and switch.

- Children change places in a line. Others guess changes.

- Hang a sheet and place a bright lamp behind it. Place various objects in front of lamp to project shadows on the sheet. Project a child's silhouette. Who is it?

Blind Trail (Touch)

up ↑ 4

Make a blind trail with string or rope, around the classroom or outside on the playground. Children walk along it blindfolded and identify specific things along the way, such as bathroom door, block corner, sink, easel, swing set, sandbox, climbing pole, etc.

Ask children to lead *each other* along the trail or guide a "blind" person around a room. Show how they might give warnings such as "steps," "curbstone," "puddle," etc.

"Braille" Another Way

up ↑ 4

- On cards draw shapes, letters, numerals, outline by gluing lentils, split peas, small buttons, etc. onto the shape. Tape a single straight object, such as a toothpick, on the lower edge in the center to indicate the bottom of the shape.

  Children wear blindfolds or close eyes and guess objects by tracing the shape with fingers.

- Trace shapes into clay. Harden and use in "Braille" games.

- Press shapes and draw figures into wet sand. Pour (1") plaster of paris over to make mold for "Braille"games.

- Cut sandpaper shapes, letters, and numerals, and glue onto cards.

Fresh Water From Salt Water (Eskimos, Multi-cultural)

up ↑ 5

Explain that Eskimos look for blocks of ice that are bluish in color. These are blocks of sea water that have frozen, melted a little and frozen again many times. Each time melting takes place, the salt slowly works its way out. Melted blue ice makes fresh drinking water. Follow up discussion with this experiment:

Fill saucepan half way with fresh water. Add three tablespoons of salt—stir—taste.

Cover a pan and boil water. Remove lid and replace it with a plate turned upside down. Allow water to cool. Taste fresh water formed on plate. (See also May—Science—*Evaporation*)

Freezing, Melting, Evaporating

up ↑ 5

Fill a one quart jar with snow. Allow to melt. Mark jar to show water level when melted. Place jar in freezer. Mark the ice line when water is frozen. Melt water and check the new level with the original water mark. Place jar on radiator and allow water to evaporate. Observe residue left when entirely evaporated. (See also May—Science—*Defrosting and Melting*)

Ice Fishing (Eskimos, Multi-cultural)

5 ↑ 3

Cut fish shapes from plastic scraps and attach a paper clip to each. Put in tub of water and set into freezer until top has a layer of ice. Break through ice and fish with magnets on string.

Snowball Experiment

up ↑ 3

Make snowballs and put in the freezer. Later, put a sheet of white construction paper under a snowball or melt in a white dish. Note the residue (dirt) left from the melted snow. A good reason not to eat snow as a general rule.

5 ↑ 3 *Snowman*

Make a small, three or four foot snowman outside. Collect additional snow in plastic buckets and bring inside to make another snowman of the same size. Set the "Silly Snowman" in the sink or container large enough to hold the melted snow. Use the following poem.

THE SILLY SNOWMAN, author unknown

Once there was a snowman
Who stood outside the door
He thought he'd like to come inside
*   And play upon the floor.*
He thought he'd like to warm himself
By the firelight red,
Thought he'd like to climb upon
*   A big white bed.*
So he called the North Wind
"Help me, Wind, I pray,
I'm completely frozen,
*   Standing out all day."*
So the North Wind came along
And blew him in the door
Now there's nothing left of him
*   But a puddle on the floor...*

up ↑ 5 *Friction*

• Put sandpaper on one side of a block of wood and rub across a board. Turn block over and rub smooth wood on same surface. Wax the smooth side of the wood and try again.

• Show how easy it is to pull a heavy load across ice or packed snow on a sled.

up ↑ 4 *Thermometer*

Thermometers "measure" temperature. Simulate indoor thermometer with red zipper sewn between two strips of cloth or a loop of bias tape fed through cardboard. Hang on the wall and label it very cold, cold, cool, warm, hot, very hot. Move zipper or tape each day to match the temperature shown on a real outside thermometer. (Also August—SCIENCE—*Temperature*)

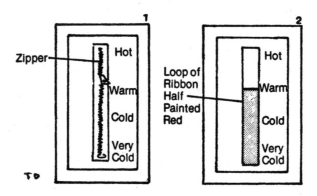

Calendar

Calendars count days and months, just as clocks count hours. Teach the basic divisions—seven days=1 week; 4-5 weeks=1 month; 12 months=1 year.

Cut old calendars and use the numbers to construct new calendars.

Place two milk cartons beside a calendar. Place a set of beans or pebbles, etc., in one carton, one for each day of the month. Remove one pebble each day and put it in the second carton. Explain that when the pebbles are all gone from the first carton, the month will be over.

Children may decide how many pebbles are needed for each month by laying one pebble on each numbered square on the calendar.

Liquid Measure (Math)

• Dramatize the necessity of measuring by deliberately shortening the juice supply in the pitcher one day. Pour full cups all around until the juice is gone and there are still empty cups. Ask: What can we do? How can we all have some? Pour all the juice back into the pitcher and re-pour, putting less in each one so that all have some. Discuss the possibilities of how to measure, using the cups and pitcher.

• Use a glass bottle as a measure. Put a strip of tape up the side. Fill with colored water. Distribute all the water into juice cups. Count, cup by cup, as water is poured back into the bottle. Mark the tape with number of cup and line of liquid, to show how much quantity increases with each cup.

• Pour the same measure of liquid into a tall, narrow bottle and into a short, wide jar. Ask: "Which has more liquid?"

• Provide children with measuring cups and milk cartons in half pint, pint, quart, half gallon and gallon sizes. Ask them to find out how many times one volume of liquid will fit into various containers (eg. 1 pint into half gallon).

Dry Measure (Math)

Do measuring activities on trays or shallow boxes for easier clean-up. Use a dry-measure cup to weigh dry substances (flour, beans, rice, sawdust, sand).

• Dry measuring containers (cup, half-cup) are accurate when contents are level with the rim. Show children how to level contents (flour, sugar, etc.) by drawing a straight edge (back of knife) across the edge.

A standard liquid measure has a space between the top measure line and the rim to allow space for liquids to move without spilling.

Dry

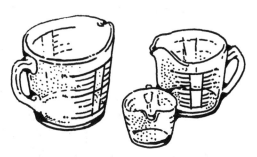

Liquid

MUSIC—MOVEMENT

up ↑ 4 Likenesses/Differences with Motions

Begin with a circle. Move all parts of the body, one at a time. Then move the whole body at one time using the following suggestions:

stiff/loose	heavy/light	slow/fast
big/small	bumpy/smooth	hot/cold

How would you express the following with your body? Use parts and then whole body.

tall/short	hopping/jumping	one foot/two feet
fat/thin	moving/stopping	one hand/two hands

5 ↑ 3 Skating

Dramatize the following poem by Deborah Mitchell Haney using motions:

SKATING TIME

We waited patiently each day

As winter came around

To take our skates down to the tree

Beside the skating pond.

> *I asked my mother, "Is it time?"*
>
> *I really couldn't wait.*
>
> *And then one day she said to me,*
>
> *"Today we'll learn to skate."*

The air was very, very cold.

The ice was very slick.

We sat beneath our little tree

And put our skates on—quick!

> *We slipped and slid across the ice*
>
> *And sometimes I would fall,*
>
> *But skating was so very nice*
>
> *It didn't hurt at all!*

5 ↑ 3 Shadow Motions

Play music. Pair children. One child shadows the other copying motions and rhythms.

up ↑ 4 Snow Dance

Children move with sliding, skating, skiing motions; walk on snowshoes; walk in deep snow. Talk about machines used in snowstorms—plows, snow blowers, snow loaders, dump trucks. Ask children to think of ways to move like machines. Several children may work together, i.e. snow loader and dump truck. Use the following variation of "Polly Wolly Doodle."

> *I can jump, jump, jump*
>
> *I can jump, jump, jump*
>
> *I can jump, jump, jump all day...etc.*

Add other motions, slide, skate, ski, shovel, etc.

LANGUAGE—DRAMA

Many language skills in this sequence involve beginning reading. It is not unusual for fives, and some fours, to be reading and writing. Early child care teachers do not attempt to "teach" these skills, but, when children ask, teachers will tell them how to spell or write a word, as is shown in the following true story.

No Blocks Today—It Happened!

Four-year-old Dick came into the classroom and saw a sheet of white paper taped over the block case. On it was printed "NO BLOCKS TODAY."

"What does that say?" he asked the teacher. She read it to him and they discussed her reasons for eliminating the blocks.

Soon Donald arrived. Taking him by the hand, Dickie pointed to the sign: "That says, NO BLOCKS TODAY," he explained. Several times more he was the giver of knowledge about this latest innovation.

Three weeks later, the sign appeared again.

"I know what that says," said Dick, "It says, NO BLOCKS TODAY."

"And that is a K," said Donald.

"That is a B," chimed Betsy, "B is in my name."

This teacher was not attempting to TEACH children to read. She was exposing them to symbols, letters with a message which had significance for them.

Story Sequences

Cut pictures from magazines, calendars, discarded story books, or use a series of drawings to illustrate stories. Tell the stories holding up pictures in sequence as they occur in the narrative. When children are familiar with the story, ask them to find and arrange the pictures in the correct order.

Use the pictures to create original stories.

Rhyming (Motions)

- Use familiar nursery and other rhymes in games. Read the rhyming words. Ask children to add new words with the same rhyming sounds.

- Make up new verses to expand familiar poems.

- Use names of the children to create a group poem. Use ideas and characteristics, favorite activities, etc. of children to describe them in the rhymes.

- Add rhyming action words and make the motions:

  "Jack, Jack, bent his back."

  "Kim, Kim, touched her chin."

  "Holly Costello, point to yellow."

Roll and Rhyme

Children sit in a circle. One rolls a ball to another and says a word—"cake." The child receiving the ball rhymes the word—"take," then rolls to another child saying a different word to start a new rhyme.

up
↑
4

Word Bag

Hang a shoe bag, or set of pockets, on the wall. Each child has a pocket. Cut cards to fit the pockets. Children, with teacher's help, record their own special words and thoughts.

Use cards for storytelling, copying, sorting, matching to pictures, etc. Some children may wish to paste pictures on one side to match the words.

5
↑
3

Chairs (Poem)

Use this poem in dramatic play.

CHAIRS by Cléa Chmela

A chair is bare   A chair at the table
Unless you sit in it.   Is never just right,
Your mother   Too high or too low
Will knit in it.   Too big or too tight.
Some chairs will rock,   Some chairs are squeezy,
But most are straight.   Wheezy and light;
Some chairs talk;   But some are called "easy"
They "squeak" with weight.   And those are just right!

5
↑
3

Cinderella

Tell the Cinderella story and dramatize with the following activity:

• Children sit in a circle. Everyone removes one shoe. Place shoes in a carton. Each child in turn takes a shoe and searches for "Cinderella" or "Prince Charming."

• Use this activity also to reinforce "Left/Right" concepts and shoe-fastening skills.

5
↑
3

Big Words

Put big words on a chart as they are introduced. As you introduce them, say each syllable slowly and dramatically.

"Co-op-er-a-tion," "fan-tas-tic", "im-a-gin-a-tion," "ex-per-i-ment," etc.

Some children may wish to copy on cards for their Word Bag pocket.

Tap the rhythms (syllables) of the words with hands, sticks, feet.

up
↑
2

Popcorn Party

Spread a clean white sheet on the floor. Set the corn popper in the center, *carefully* securing the cord to prevent tripping.

Children sit around the edge of the cloth in front of a sheet of newspaper with his/her name on it.

Before starting the popper, warn children that the popcorn will be hot when it is first popped. Also, "Eat only the pieces which fall on your newspaper."

Start the popper—DO NOT USE THE LID—the popping corn will fly all around the area. Teacher should watch to be sure popcorn is evenly distributed.

• Use this activity to observe language. Encourage many different ways to describe the motion, sound, smell and excitement of the event.

• Later, use the idea to develop a "Corn Popping" movement session with the children becoming the kernels of corn. (See following true story.)

Popcorn People—It Happened

In one center, a director heard a terrible thumping and squealing coming through the ceiling. In dismay, she went charging upstairs to quiet the explosion of classroom noise. The class had just had fun with popcorn. Following the spontaneous reaction of one exuberant four-year-old, all the children and teachers were "being" popcorn. The director, too, was soon bouncing and jumping around on the "hot" floor as she became a kernel of corn being popped into a fluffy white piece of popcorn.

CREATIVE PROJECTS

Child's Room (Language Development)

* Children make large posters with pictures of things in their rooms. Use catalogs and magazines for pictures of furnishings, toys, clothing, books, etc.

* Vary the activity: Ask child to close eyes and describe his/her room.

* Ask one child to describe any room in a house. Others guess which room.

Scrapbook House (On-going Project)

Make individual scrapbook houses. Covers might be cut from cardboard in the shape of a house. Bind books with string so books will lie flat and pages will turn easily. Wallpaper sample books are a good resource.

Each page represents a room in the house. Child pastes pictures of furnishings.

Decorate walls with windows, pictures, clocks, etc. Put rugs on floors and hang fixtures from the ceiling.

Decorate covers (outside of houses) with shrubs, windows, doors. Add the child's address.

Use paper doll families with Scrapbook House.

JUST FOR FUN

Paper Snow Balls

Crumple snowballs from newspaper. Cover with tissue and secure with masking tape. Roll and push with noses and sticks. Play snowball hockey and baseball using small brooms. Toss into baskets.

TODDLERS, TOO!

Scavenger Hunt

Paste five to ten pictures on cards showing familiar objects found in the building. Children choose cards and find the objects. Older children can work in teams.

Fashion Show

Display an assortment of clothing—warm and cold weather items; costumes from other cultures; hats; work clothing; uniforms. Children dress up to solve various problems:

"You are traveling to a cold climate." "You have just arrived from Mexico." "You work in an auto repair shop."

Use paper dolls and clothing pictures in the same way.

THE CHILD is gradually led through the world of PEOPLE from his own egocentric concept to a broader realization of where he fits into the total scheme of "peopleness".

SEQUENCE SIX

FEBRUARY

FEBRUARY THEMES

FEBRUARY

Pillow Fights and Loving Hearts

Angry, angry, angry,
So angry that I kick the air!
And stamp my feet and pull my hair.
Now isn't it curious
That after feeling so furious,
I feel very good once more?
(From *Emotions*, Anonymous)

People need people, a child needs a **friend**, a friend is someone to love. The **emotions** of **love** and **hate** are opposites. Our **faces** reflect the many emotions we feel in between love and hate. **Valentines** express our feelings of love and friendship.

Doctors, nurses and **emergency** people help to make us well in **hospitals** and clinics. **Presidents** and other **leaders** help to govern.

People live in **neighborhoods** and villages where they learn to trust and respect each other and understand differences. Who lives in your apartment building or next door that you can ask to help you in an emergency—who has a Safe House?

Activities encourage children to be curious, to ask questions. We must also protect them when curiosity and exploration lead them into danger, such as "What is in the **medicine closet**?"

We encourage children to conserve paper and appreciate other products from trees such as **maple syrup**. Some may be able to visit a sugar house, others can read about the process of boiling down the water-like sap into golden brown syrup.

"Hurry up Spring!" Bring some "sunshine" inside when you **force blooms** of "bright yellow bows, tied up in rows" along a stem of forsythia.

Science activities explore and suggest **sound** experiments. Children use **real stethoscopes** to hear heartbeats.

Motions using colorful **scarves, body "language,"** facial expressions and dramatic play help children explore their feelings. Songs, stories and poems about **friends** and **enemies** can help children be comfortable with strong feelings.

There are many ways to create red, **pink, lavender,** and **lacy valentines** that say "I love you."

Energy and emotions come together—JUST FOR FUN!—in relay races, obstacle courses and...a Camouflage Hunt?

SEQUENCE SIX

PEOPLE

up ↑ 3 *Friends and Enemies*

Discuss friendship. What does it mean to be a friend? Am I a friend? Why do we like our friends? Talk about being your own friend, taking care of one's self, self-respect, self-love.

When talking about friends, allow time also for talk about enemies. What makes you get angry? What makes you get mad at your best friend? Why do you like your friend? How do you feel when you aren't chosen?

up ↑ 4 *The President*

Ask: "Who is the president? What do presidents do and where do they live?" Look for the names of past presidents on signs, money, stamps and on maps. Point out street names and public buildings named for presidents. Older children might discuss the differences between presidents, kings, emperors and dictators.

up ↑ 3 *Doctors and Nurses*

- What do doctors and nurses do? Where?

- What kinds of things do they use? If possible, have the real items; if not, show pictures of a stethoscope, thermometer, Ace bandage, etc.

- Encourage the children to ask questions and talk about their experiences with doctors and nurses.

up ↑ 4 *Emergency Squad*

Who are they? Ambulance drivers, policemen, firemen, paramedics.

What equipment do they use? Ambulances, rescue trucks, sirens, stretchers, oxygen tanks, radios.

What is an emergency? List and show pictures: fire, drowning, falling from high places. Ask children to relate their own experiences. Review telephone (9-1-1) skills.

EXPANDING OUR WORLD

up ↑ 3 *Hospital*

- Ask children about their hospital experiences and write a story based on their responses. Where did you sleep? Did your parent stay with you? Did visitors come to see you? What and where did you eat? Where were the bathrooms? Did you have medicine? Needles?

- Help children remember the positive experiences, i.e. "You had pain but it went away." "You were lonesome but people came to visit." "You were brave." "Hospital people helped you to get better."

up ↑ 3 *Hospital Play*

After reading the following true experience, encourage dramatic play by providing equipment that will set things rolling: stethoscope, stretcher, bandages, white shirts with sleeves cut short, etc.

The Hospital—It Happened! (Dramatic Play)

The interest center where housekeeping play usually took place was transformed with the addition of a few simple props. The children needed no discussion about the changes—they simply followed the cues suggested by the new items they discovered.

A low bed, made from a cot and covered with a white sheet, became the "examination and operating room." White mens' shirts, with sleeves cut short, hung on hooks. A *real* stethoscope, doctors' headbands, pen lights, small bottles and pill boxes, Ace bandages and strips of sheeting, cotton balls and throat sticks were set out on a vanity table.

"Doctor Williams," a five-year-old, put on a white smock and headband and hovered over a patient at the operating table. "Dr. Murphy," his colleague, finished giving a shot. "When you leave the hospital, hang your uniform on the hook," she directed.

Two girls and a boy, in smocks, were tending to sick dolls in a ward of beds, made from seatblocks. "Mrs. Leonard has a fever, she needs some water and two of these pills," Jessie said with a serious expression of concern. Nurses Carrie and Brian took temperatures and wrapped another doll's arm in a bandage. Dr. Murphy used her stethoscope to check Rebecca's heartbeat.

Throughout the following weeks, the walls were filled with pictures and collages created from throat sticks, cotton balls, Q-tips and tape.

At another center, the teacher explained, referring to a group of school-age children who had set up a similar hospital following the illness of one of their friends..."This activity has been going on for over a week every afternoon when they arrive after school. I stay nearby, in case I am needed, but I don't "teach" or direct. These children do not need adults hovering over them. When they arrive in mid-afternoon they have had enough "teaching" for one day."

Neighborhood/Village

Explore your center's neighborhood. Use *different* walks to ask children such questions as:

- Which buildings do people live in? How many families might live there? (Single home/apartment)

- Which are stores? What can we buy here? (Food? Clothing? Gasoline? Building supplies? Books? Toys?)

- Look for places to play. (Playgrounds, parks)

- Look for places where help or services might be given. (Police or fire station, clinic, hospital, library, bank, repair shops, cleaners.)

- Ask children to describe their own neighborhoods. Collect pictures to make "My Neighborhood" books.

- With SCHOOL AGE children, talk about the differences between yard, neighborhood, village, town, city.

SKILLS FOR DAILY LIVING

Putting Toys Away

Children should be taught from the beginning to put things away. Review these skills often, giving more responsibility to the group as the year progresses.

- *Make it easy.* Use plastic dishpans as bins for various plastic put-together sets. Glue one piece (or use a picture) on the end of the bin and put another picture on the shelf where that bin goes.

- *Give a warning signal* five minutes before it is time to stop play. Quietly go to each group. Show cardboard clock face. "When the long hand is here on the wall clock, we will stop and put everything away."

- *Allow enough time.* If you want to go out at 10:45, start clean-up by 10:30.

- *Make a game of it.* Hold up a piece. "Which bin does this go in? How many more like this can you find?"

5 ↑ 3 | *Pillow Fights (Emotional Health)*

Set up a "soft" area with carpet and soft wall coverings. Add a collection of small pillows. When two children have a disagreement, invite them to have a pillow fight and turn anger and frustration into giggles.

Suggested rules:

Only two children at a time.

Time limit (3 to 5 minutes). Set an alarm clock.

Always leave with a grin at each other.

up ↑ 4 | *Medicine Closet*

Discuss the dangers and the positive uses of medicine. Perhaps each child could make a DANGER poster to put on the medicine chest at home. This might serve as a reminder to parents to then check the contents of cabinet and secure toxic items with a lock.

CONCEPTS

up ↑ 4 | *Late/On Time*

- Using a clock face, set the hands to show twelve o'clock. Say to the group, "Lunch is at twelve o'clock, when the clock looks like this. What if we went for a walk and didn't come back till *this* time?" (Show one o'clock.) "That's right. Lunch would be over—the food would be all gone—and we would go hungry! All because we were *LATE!* If we had been here by twelve, we would have been *ON TIME.*"

- Ask if they have ever had a problem because they were late? When is it *most* important to be on time? (Catching buses, trains, planes) How can they be sure to be on time for things?

5 ↑ 3 | *Pink*

Pink is often used for valentines. There are many shades of pink.

- Look for pink in the children's clothing.

- Have a Pink Search. Look around the center for pink things.

- Provide samples of cloth, thread, yarn, etc. in different shades of pink. Ask the children to arrange them. Will they sort by shades, lights and darks, or by materials and textures?

5 ↑ 3 | *Hearts Are for Love*

Hold up a paper heart. "This is not really the way the heart in your body looks, but it is the shape that stands for love and friendship. Valentines are usually heart-shaped. Watch for hearts in decorations and pictures, especially during February."

SCIENCE

up ↑ 3 — *No-sugar/Low-sugar Snacks*

• *Presentation is important.* Use whole-wheat bread cut in triangles instead of squares to offer these spreads:

Peanut butter can be mixed with one or several of the following:

grated carrots	raisins
cut-up dates	cut-up prunes
diced bananas	chopped apples

• Individual paper nut cups filled with any (or a mixture of) fresh berries: blueberries, raspberries, strawberries. Watch for off-season (winter) "specials" on fresh berries.

• Arrange star burst and other designs with carrot sticks and celery sticks, etc..

up ↑ 3 — *Animal Camouflage*

One of the ways nature helps animals protect themselves is by camouflage. This means they blend into the background. For example, polar bears live where there is always snow, so nature gave them white fur—it is hard to see them in the snow.

Some animals, like snowshoe hares (a kind of rabbit) and a bird called a ptarmigan change colors. In the summer, they are brown; in the winter, they turn white. Chameleons are small lizards that change color to match whatever they are on.

• Show children pictures of camouflaged animals.

• Scatter about 100 colored toothpicks in the grass. (Know how many of each color you had.) Give the children a set amount of time to try to find them. They will discover that it is a lot easier to find the red and yellow ones than the green.

• Cut out animals like tiger, giraffe, zebra, rabbit, beaver, etc. Ask the children to color them, using pictures as examples. One group hides the animals outside by "camouflage." A second group finds them.

up ↑ 2 — *Forcing Spring*

Cut some forsythia and pussy willow branches. Put them in water and force the blooms. Count the number of days it takes until buds open.

up ↑ 3 — *Pool Garden*

Plant an indoor garden in a small, plastic swimming pool. Later, transplant the seedlings outside. Marigolds and petunias are hardy seedlings.

up ↑ 3 — *Maple Trees/Syrup*

Show pictures and read books which describe the process of making maple syrup.

Tap a maple tree. What is a spile?

Visit a sugar house to see maple syrup production. (Northern states)

Serve maple syrup on ice cream; taste maple sugar.

February

up
↑
3

Sound Pictures

- Make a set of pictures of objects that make a sound, such as typewriter, bus, dog, etc. Hold up pictures and ask children to make the appropriate sound. Reverse activity by having one child make a particular sound, and others find picture to match sound.

- Make a tape recording of some sounds and use with pictures.

up
↑
4

Ears Can Tell

Collect a number of objects of metal, glass, plastic, wood. Show each one; name it; let children handle and experiment with sounds.

Later, put objects on a table behind a screen. One child goes behind screen and uses combination of objects to create sounds. (Spoon tapping glass, paper crumpling, etc.) Other children guess how the sounds were made.

up
↑
3

Stethoscope

Use a real stethoscope to listen to heartbeats. Feel pulses. Listen to heart beats of a small animal. Discuss the heart, comparing it to a pump.

Compare rate of heartbeat when quiet and after running and jumping.

up
↑
4

Vibrations Amplified

Tie two pieces of string, each about 12 inches long, to corners of a rack from a refrigerator or oven. Hold strings in each hand and put a finger in each ear. Lean forward slightly so rack can swing free, not touching the body.

Another person rubs and *gently* strikes the rack with various objects (spoons, dowels, pencils).

The vibrations of sound will travel through the string.

Refrigerator
Rack

up
↑
3

Vocal Sounds

Speak, whisper, shout, whistle—indoors, in large spaces, in closets or small closed rooms.

Go outside and repeat in large open areas, under porch roofs and trees, in wooded places. Make paper cones from cardboard (megaphones) and repeat the same sounds. Compare.

up
↑
5

Sound Chamber

Drape a cloth over a table or large carton. Create sounds inside. Replace cloth with cardboard covers. Note difference in sounds.

Put a plastic cup up to an ear and hold the other end against the table surface. Child underneath makes sounds. The cup will amplify the sounds. Do the same experiment holding the cup against a wall between rooms.

up
↑
5

Fog and Steam

How does fog feel and smell? What makes the fog? Clouds are floating fog. Have you ever flown through a cloud or driven through fog? Can we make fog? What happens when you open the freezer door on a warm day? Read Carl Sandburg's *Fog*.

How is steam different from fog? Can we make steam? Demonstrate with a whistling teakettle. Blow up a balloon and release the air. Relate it to the way the water in the kettle boils and pushes air through the kettle's whistle. Steam works for us. Show pictures of steam trains, steam iron, pressure cookers.

To demonstrate steam and fog, fill a pyrex jar half full of boiling water. Cover jar and put an ice cube on the lid. Observe results.

MUSIC-MOVEMENT

| 5 |
| ↑ |
| 3 |

Do You Know This Friend of Mine? (Friends)
(Tune: Oh, Do You Know the Muffin Man?)

Oh, do you know this friend of mine?

This friend of mine, this friend of mine?

Oh, do you know this friend of mine?

His name is Geor-gie Lincoln.

> *Oh, yes, we know this friend of yours,*
>
> *This friend of yours, this friend of yours,*
>
> *Oh, yes, we know this friend of yours,*
>
> *His name is Geor-gie Lincoln.*

| up |
| ↑ |
| 5 |

Emotion Motions
Show pictures depicting various emotions. Ask children what sound they would make to show a particular feeling. How would you move? Ask the children to move the way the picture makes them feel.

Ask children, "Show me how you would move if: you lost a puppy; you had broken your mother's best dish; you saw your brother playing with your toy after you told him not to; your mother had been away for a whole week and you saw her coming in the door."

| 5 |
| ↑ |
| 3 |

Ladders
With four foot ladders placed flat on the floor, ask children how many ways they can think of to walk on them. Through rungs, hopping or jumping? On rungs? On edges? One edge? Use drum to accompany children's movements. Play follow the leader on the ladder.

| 5 |
| ↑ |
| 3 |

Scarves
- Sit in a circle. Each child chooses a chiffon, nylon or net scarf. Explore the color and shape. Practice folding into squares and rectangles.

- Ask each child to make a motion for others to copy.

- Play music and ask children to move around using the scarves in dance motion. Lie on backs and sit on chairs to make scarf motions.

- Ask child to think of different ways to wear the scarves.

- Toss the scarves, catch them; let the scarves fall and make designs on the floor; toss scarves to someone else.

- Arrange the scarves in a rainbow of color.

- At the end of scarf play, ask each child to fold and put the scarf in its storage container.

February

up ↑ 4 Instrument Sounds (Sensory Game)

Display and demonstrate five familiar musical instruments—big and small bells, drum, shaker, tambourine. Choose five children to go out of sight and ask each one to play an instrument. Children in the group try to guess which instrument was played.

up ↑ 4 I Want to be a Friend of Yours (Friends)

Sit in a circle. Put a basket of valentines in the center. First child chooses a valentine and skips around the outside of the circle as the song is sung and drops the valentine in back of someone before the song stops.

At the end of the song, all turn to see who has the valentine. That child puts the valentine in front of him/her and then chooses a valentine from the basket to give to another child as the song is sung again.

When all the children have a valentine, the game ends.

> I want to be a friend of yours
>> Mmmm and a little bit more
>
> I want to be a pal of yours
>> Mmmm and a little bit more
>
> I want to be a little flower
>> Growing round your door
>
> I want to be your mother, father, sister, brother
>> Mmmm and a little bit more.

LANGUAGE—DRAMA

up ↑ 3 Valentines

Discuss heart, love, heart throb, heart beat with the children. Ask why and to whom we send messages of love on Valentine's Day. List the words/ideas of the children and use for creating valentines. Some suggestions for valentines follow in the Creative Projects section. Remember, the fun is in the making, not the product!

up ↑ 5 Facial Expressions and Body Language

Our body language tells much about our thoughts, feelings, moods and emotions. Help children know others and themselves by exploring body language.

- Faces say, "Hello. Come talk to me." Or, "Leave me alone, I feel sad." Eyelids can alter communication just by being lowered. Mouths indicate moods by the turn of their corners, which can be thin and tight or expand into a smile.

- Bodies "talk," too. Heads nod, shoulders slump, feet tap.

Look at pictures of people and notice their body posture and the position of hands and feet. Look for pictures about happy things. Look for pictures that show sadness.

up ↑ 5 Faces Collage

- Collect pictures of all kinds of faces depicting emotions, ages and races of people, to assemble as a collage. Listen to the children talk about the pictures as they choose them, cut them and paste them.

Hospital Mural

- Collect pictures relating to hospitals and illness and assemble as a mural.

- Write the children's comments in "speech bubbles" (as in cartoons).

- Talk together about the differences between people who are ill and people who are *physically challenged*, i.e. in wheelchairs, on crutches, hearing/speech/sight impaired, with braces, etc. "These people are not ill, they are *physically challenged*" (instead of "handicapped").

Ten Little Monkeys

Ten little monkeys jumping on the bed.

One fell off and hurt his head.

Called the doctor and the doctor said,

"No more monkeys jumping on the bed."

CREATIVE PROJECTS

Village on a Table (Spatial Concept)

Children use assorted boxes, tubes, plastic containers to construct houses, garages, schools, churches, shops, factories, etc. and assemble in a village on a table. Paste doors, windows, shrubs, signs, and addresses on the buildings.

Children add pieces of black, green and blue paper for roads, grass and water. With cardboard and tape they can add standing street signs, trees, flag poles, etc.

They can also hang tubes under the table to represent water (grey), sewer (black/white) and gas lines (yellow). Strings and wires run through some tubes or straws can represent underground electric lines.

Auto Factory

<table>
<tr><td>up
↑
5</td></tr>
</table>

- Offer a box of paper circles, squares, ovals and rectangles which children can use to construct pasted pictures of cars and trucks.
- Collect small boxes, tubes, washers, dowels, telephone wire, tape, paper fasteners, etc. for constructing 3-dimensional vehicles.
- Paste pictures of vehicles on folded cardboard "tents" to stand up around the "factory" (table) for use as models.

SCHOOL AGE

Faces From Clay

- Use several colors of clay for flesh, hair, and other body tones.
- Give children oval-shaped heavy paper on which they create faces with the clay. Begin with flesh outline/shape; add features and hair, etc. from other colors.

Self Portraits and Silhouettes

- Use mirrors to experiment with making faces. When children have discovered how they look when they are happy, sad, angry, etc., ask them to draw pictures of themselves in various moods.
- Focus a spotlight or bright lamp to shine on a sheet of drawing paper hung on a wall or easel. Children sit so their silhouette shadow is cast onto the paper. Teacher draws around the shadow outline.
- Cut around silhouettes and mount on paper of a contrasting color.

Thumbprint Hearts

- Dip each thumb (up to first knuckle) into (red, pink, purple) paint and print on paper so the two prints touch making a heart-shape.
- Press the entire hand print. Cut out and tape two hands together to make a Valentine folder.
- Tape hand prints on child's silhouette. Decorate with thumbprint hearts.

TODDLERS, TOO!

Wax Valentines

Cut two heart shapes from wax paper. Grate crayons and mix chips with confetti. Sprinkle on one heart, cover with second heart, *waxed sides together.* Lay between sheets of brown paper and press with a warm iron until wax melts. Children staple or glue on ribbon hangers.

Old-Fashioned Valentines

- Show samples of old-fashioned valentines.
- Mix red paint into shades of pink. Paint on paper and cut into hearts.
- Decorate hearts with lace doilies, trims, stickers and shiny sequins.

Confetti Valentines

Dip brushes or Q-tips in thinned glue/water solution and draw pictures or designs on colored hearts. Lay on a tray and shake on confetti.

JUST FOR FUN

Valentine Box Game
$\begin{array}{c}5\\\uparrow\\3\end{array}$

- Decorate a box with pink and red hearts, lace, foil, stickers, crêpe paper, cloth, smiling faces, etc. Cut a slot in the top for "mailing" valentines.

- Each child "mails" a heart (no name). Add some extras.

- Take turns pulling out hearts and giving them to friends until everyone has a valentine.

- Use the same hearts several times, returning them to the box after all are delivered. At the *end* of a Valentine Party, each child chooses a heart from the box to take home with others he/she has made.

Obstacle Courses
$\begin{array}{c}5\\\uparrow\\3\end{array}$

Set up "over," "under," "around," "between," etc. obstacle courses using furniture, cartons, ladders, cones, ropes, blanket tents, etc.

Introduce a stop watch or timer to add to the excitement.

Magazine Relay
$\begin{array}{c}up\\\uparrow\\5\end{array}$

Put two piles of magazines in front of two teams. Leader calls out the name of a familiar object. First child in each line hunts through the magazines for the object. First one to find it wins a point for the team. Vary the game for younger children by pasting the pictures onto oak tag and placing them in two boxes. Child finds the picture in the box.

Relay Races
$\begin{array}{c}up\\\uparrow\\3\end{array}$

- Heart on a straw—Carry a small cardboard heart by sucking it up against a straw.

- Paper stamp—Give each player two sheets of paper, numbered 1 and 2. Form two lines, first in line put No. 1 down, step on it, put No. 2 down, step on No. 2, pick up No. 1, etc.

- Potato/ball on a spoon—Carry a potato or tennis ball on a spoon.

- Egg carton—Place twelve small objects at one end of a course, egg carton at the other. Players carry one object at a time until carton is full.

Variation: Place a pile of pictures which match the egg carton objects beside the carton. Child chooses a picture, runs to find the object, races back to put it in the carton.

Camouflage Hunt, Indoors
$\begin{array}{c}up\\\uparrow\\3\end{array}$

The object is to "hide" objects in plain sight by blending them into the background. With the younger children, show them what will be hidden, hide them while they are out of the room. Examples: a small brown teddy bear on a brown blanket, a red Lego piece taped to red construction paper on the wall, a shiny quarter taped to a silver doorknob, an unwrapped green crayon standing in a flowerpot with a green plant. Hide only 4-5 objects.

As the children get older, objects become smaller. For 10-12 year olds in after school programs, use more difficult items—paper clips, matches, buttons, birthday candles, etc.

Explain that in order not to "give away" the hiding place they must move away from the object before they write down where it is. When they have found all the objects, they show the list to the teacher to make sure their answers are correct (e.g., paper clips in a box on the teacher's desk would not be correct).

LEARNING takes place as a child interacts with his world, and becomes a part of the action. Learning is exciting! The child who can add "I know!" to his "I AM" and "I CAN" senses fulfillment.

SEQUENCE SEVEN

MARCH

MARCH THEMES

MARCH

Babies Sprouting—Siblings Pouting

Babies, born all through the year, are an endless source of fascination. "Baby" also needs lots of attention and care from parents. Siblings, especially young ones, feel left out, jealous and even angry about the baby. How can we help children cope with *sibling rivalry*? What is it like to be the baby? Can baby run, eat without help, roll the ball like *I* can?

Many *animal babies* are born during *springtime. Chicks, ducklings, turtles* and *birds hatch* from eggs. *Ant farms* and nests come alive with young. All of nature bursts with *new growth* in the spring. The sun shines a little longer and feels warmer. Adults and children who have been forced to stay inside during wintry days are bursting with energy. Like new *buds and shoots*, young children spurt with growth and itch to go outside.

The natural world, all year long, is an *outside classroom*, but during springtime the world outside becomes a laboratory for learning (in all *shades of green*!). Plan inside and outside activities and observe how children *learn through play*, always keeping in mind that "play is the work" of children.

Fathers' and mothers' work includes a great variety of *occupations*. Factories and offices, shops and garages use *machines* and *tools*. A machine can be as simple as a pencil or as complex as its sharpener. Occupations use complex machines like computers and *simple machines* like screw drivers to put them together. Children can experiment with and sort some of the different kinds of machines: *levers, pulleys, wedges, inclined planes, wheels and axles*.

Machines collect and *recycle* trash. Children can help sort recyclable items, learning ways to be responsible for their environment. Sprucing up the housekeeping area—washing and drying doll's clothes—are *skills* children can learn to take care of their environment.

During March we can grow *sprouts* for soups and salads; plant seeds; look for clover and make *shamrock (clover)* shapes with circles; nibble *carrots* like *baby bunnies*; look for *pussy willows*.

March activities suggest ways to make and use *rattles* and *shakers* in motion games. Children can turn cartons into *turtle* shells and pom poms into bunny tails. Spring themes offer new ways to make up *alphabet rhymes*, books and songs.

Jobs, work and play activities are done in a certain order, a *sequence*. Which thing do we do first? What comes next? What do we do last?

And—JUST FOR FUN!—of course, we can "butter up," compliment, cajole, and tease each other with a bit o' *Blarney*.

SEQUENCE SEVEN

PEOPLE

5 ↑ 3 *Babies*

- Discuss and show pictures of babies of all kinds, human and animal. Talk about eggs and chicks, nesting and nursing. How are animal babies alike or different from human babies in size, weight and development? Discuss differences in the way animals and humans take care of their babies.

- Ask children to bring in baby pictures of themselves. Display on a bulletin board with a recent picture of each child. Include teacher baby pictures.

5 ↑ 3 *Baby Care*

Some children have no babies at home. If it can be arranged, invite them to a special demonstration of bathing, dressing and feeding a real baby. Let them help in as many ways as they can. Before and after the demonstration, talk through the steps using a doll.

up ↑ 3 *I Can! Baby Can't!*

Hold discussions about what your children can do that babies cannot. List on charts and add pictures. (Baby creeping—child walking, etc.) This is a great ego booster for older brothers and sisters who are feeling "left out."

5 ↑ 3 *Baby Party*

Invite mothers and fathers and babies to a party. Serve pudding or jello to the older children and possibly to some of the babies. Tape sounds the babies make.

After visiting babies leave, discuss all the special attention they required, the time it took, the regular group activities that were left out in order to care for the babies. This might help children to understand the extra time and attention babies need from the mother and father.

EXPANDING OUR WORLD

up ↑ 3 *Parents' Occupations*

- Discuss the various occupations of parents. Invite parents to come and talk to the children about their work, showing tools, special equipment used, and pictures of their office or factory and of people at work there.

- Arrange, if possible, to visit parents' places of employment. Make word and picture cards for each job. Following the trip, invite different workers to visit and describe duties showing special tools, machines, etc. used in their work.

up ↑ 3 *Greenhouse/Nursery*

- Visit a greenhouse or tree nursery to see machines used for soil preparation, sifting, fertilizing and planting.

- Visit to see plants, full grown and seedlings (baby plants) in various stages of growth. Arrange to go at a time when someone will be free to show the children around and answer questions.

- Bring back a large plant from which to make cuttings, or, depending on planting time in your area, seedlings to plant.

Machines at Work

Visit a place where simple and complex machines do their daily work. For example:

Construction sites where bulldozers dig and lift. (Levers and pulleys)

Docks where cranes load and unload ships. (Levers and pulleys)

Saw mills and woodworking shops which cut and plane boards. (Wedges)

Loading platforms that move supplies on ramps and elevators. (Inclined plane)

Irrigation sluices that funnel water; screws and gears which raise and lower dam gates. (Wheels & axles)

Sand pits that sort stones on chutes, belts and ramps. (Inclined planes; wheel & axle)

Houses on the move and service stations where cars are lifted on jackscrews. (Wheel & axle; screw)

Cider mills which use presses. (Screw)

SKILLS FOR DAILY LIVING

 ### *Recycling*

Aluminum is the material which is most efficiently recycled. New aluminum can be made from old with very little loss.

Glass, ground up and melted down to make new glass, comes next in recycling efficiency.

Plastic comes from petroleum, used also to make the gasoline that runs cars.

Metals come from ores and can be recycled to make cars, toys and machines.

Paper comes from trees. When we recycle paper to make more, we save trees.

- Very young children can be taught to sort trash into the right bins. Use a magnet to sort steel from aluminum.

- Older children can begin to make the connections explained above.

- Arrange for someone in local recycling programs to talk to the children and give recognition for their help. Some local conservation groups give certificates.

 ### *Laundry/Spring Housecleaning*

If your center has a washer/dryer:

- Set up a "laundromat" where children can wash, rinse, dry, sort and fold doll's clothes, dress-ups, blankets and other cloth items in the housekeeping center.

- Put soapy water in the sink for children to wash doll dishes.

- Wash toys. Launder cuddlies in washer, teach children to measure the soap.

- Sort, wash, dry and display any washable "Lost and Found" clothing. Put unclaimed items in a box to take to a Goodwill center. Tell children this is another way to recycle useful items.

- Use unmatched gloves, mittens and socks to create puppets. Give them names which will remind the children they came from recycled items:

>   Dust Bin Willie
>
>   Tossed Away Tina
>
>   Second-hand Hannah

March

up ↑ 3 *Teeth*

Children who learn good dental habits when they are three will have strong, white teeth later on.

- By the sink, provide a rack to hold each child's labeled toothbrush. Brushing takes place after snacks and meals.

- Children four and up can be taught how to floss. Dentists advise flossing as a very important step in keeping teeth healthy.

- Ask your dentist, a dental clinic, or a toothpaste company for charts and posters about teeth.

- Most dentists will give you disclosing tablets which the children chew. When they rinse their mouths, the red color will wash off except where there is plaque. Children can look in a mirror and see exactly where they need to brush more thoroughly.

up ↑ 2 *Turtles and Salmonella*

Most people associate salmonella with eggs, not realizing that it can also be passed by turtles. Stress to children that they must be sure to wash hands after handling turtles.

CONCEPTS

5 ↑ 3 *Light/Heavy*

Put out an assortment of light and heavy items: cork, styrofoam ball, cotton balls, feather, balloon, brick, log, gallon jug full of water, iron pan, five lb. bag of flour, etc. Children sort items into light and heavy.

5 ↑ 3 *Green*

Children look for green things and arrange them on a table. Together they count and sort the different shades.

- Children mix blue and yellow paint to make green, experimenting with the two basic colors to get different shades of green.

- Teach older children various words for green: emerald, jade, aqua, etc. Look for color shade names on decorating charts, paint chips, names on threads, crayons and markers, wall paper samples, etc. Try to find samples to go with the different words.

- Go for a walk with the children and bring back natural shades of green—grass, leaves from trees and plants, pine needles, moss, etc. Bring only a few of each kind (ecology!).

5 ↑ 3 *Cylinders*

Put out an assortment of hollow cylinders (pipes, tubing, straws, toilet paper tubes) and solid cylinders (dowel, crayon, rolling pin). As children sort, talk about how the cylinders are alike and different. Use the word *cylinder* often.

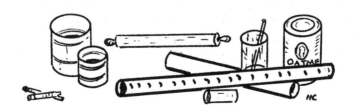

SCIENCE

up ↑ 2 ***Green Food (Multi-cultural)***
In honor of St. Patrick's Day, serve a completely green meal. Choose from lettuce, celery or pea soup, olives, artichokes, limes, green gelatin and sherbet, green beans, broccoli, mint jelly, cole slaw, green grapes.

Serve green eggs and read *Green Eggs and Ham* by Dr. Seuss (pub. Random House). Serve pistachio ice cream. Read *Pistachio* by Blair Lent (pub. Little Brown)

up ↑ 2 ***Sprout Soup***
Make chicken or beef flavored bouillon and add sprouts, rice or noodles, sautéed onions and/or other finely chopped vegetables.

up ↑ 2 ***Carrots***
Cut into new shapes for snacks—diced, triangles, crinkles, rounds. (Cook carrots slightly for toddlers, to prevent choking.)

up ↑ 2 ***Chicks Born in Class—It Happened!***

In one school a large incubator was installed and the eggs were watched carefully and anxiously for several days. It was important to plan the timing so eggs would hatch while the children were present, on a weekday.

At last the day came! The hatching went on all day. Children took turns watching as baby chicks pecked their way out of the shells. They emerged all wet and scrawny, gradually changing in appearance as they dried. The children heard the cracking shells and the tiny cheeps. It was a thrilling experience for teachers as well as children.

Note: Before planning such an adventure, arrange for a home for the babies. Some hatcheries will loan hatchlings and take them back as well as provide the necessary equipment and advice.

up ↑ 3 ***Animal Babies (Matching)***
Make cards with pictures of baby animals and cards of their parents. Match baby animal with its parent. Use for following games which progress in difficulty.

a.   Put out cards in sets, name the animals, then ask children to name them.

b.   Mix cards, lay out face up. Children take turns picking out a parent–baby set.

c.   Mix cards. Turn over, lay out in rows. Play as Concentration. Child turns up two cards. A match gives another turn. Children test memory skills as they find matches and make sets.

up ↑ 3 ***Ant Farm***
Fill a one gallon jar, or similar large, glass container, with soil. Find an ant hill. Shovel the surrounding dirt and debris into jar. Cover the jar with dark paper to encourage the ants to make tunnels. Place some cotton on top of the dirt and pour a little water on it every few days. Feed the ants crumbs of bread and cookies, honey or sugar water.

March

Sprouts

Grow edible sprouts from seeds—alfalfa, almonds, barley, beans, buckwheat, corn, lentils, etc.

- Wash seeds and place in a bowl of warm water—four cups water to one cup seeds. Soak overnight and drain.
- Put seeds in a sprouting container such as a one quart glass jar. Cover with cheesecloth or nylon netting. Drain excess water, put in a warm, dark area with even temperature.
- Rinse and drain twice daily.

Sprouts will appear in two or three days and are ready to eat when seeds have opened and sprout is well developed. Serve in salads, soups, omelets, breads and cakes. Some experiments:

- Demonstrate the different ways to cause germination.
    - a. Place between wet blotters. Keep well watered for seven to ten days.
    - b. Place around the sides of a glass jar which has wet cotton in the center (cotton keeps the seeds against the sides for better viewing).
    - c. Place seeds in a jar of water. Some submerged, some above water.
- Put one of each of these growing suggestions in different conditions: full sun; dark closet; refrigerator; outside.
- Observe and chart (children draw illustrations or find picture of mature plant):
    - a. which germinates first (use several kinds)
    - b. which need water
    - c. which need sun (or will germinate in dark-underground)
    - d. which need air (those under water "suffocate")

Clover

- Plant clover seeds. Look for Shamrock in St. Patrick's Day decorations. Find clover growing.
- Press clover leaves between wax paper sheets. Attach green ribbon ties and wear as good luck charms.

MACHINES

There are six categories of simple machines. Some machines we call tools. The six simple machines are the *lever*, the *inclined plane*, the *pulley*, the *screw*, the *wheel and axle*, and the *wedge*.

Tools

- Display some common hand tools and teach their names—screw driver, hammer, scissors, egg beater, plier, knife, tire iron.
- Demonstrate and practice using some of the tools in simple tasks.
- Draw around tools. Ask children to identify by the outlines.
- Make charts which show tools and pictures of the work/jobs for which they are used.

Levers

One of the oldest tools used by humans—a tree branch prying a rock—is a lever, as are hammers, crowbars, can openers, seesaws, pliers, scissors, hinges, shovels and oars.

- Put some blocks in a box. Try to lift it. Use a broom handle and a pile of blocks as a fulcrum. Now try to lift the box using the broom handle leverage.

- Put the box on one end of a board balanced like a seesaw. Lift the box by pushing down on the opposite end.

- Open a can of juice; drive a nail; dig a hole in sand with shovel or fingers. The can opener, the hammer, the shovel and fingers are all levers.

Tongs and Tweezers (Levers)

Strengthen the small muscles of hands, fingers and wrists with a series of activities using tongs of many sizes. This activity can be planned as a progressive series for each age group.

a. Salad tongs (one hand)—serve foods, picking up large items.

b. Fire tongs (two hands)—pick up large items such as blocks or empty boxes.

c. Snap clothes pins—(one hand, fingers)—hang items on a line.

d. Push clothes pins—(one hand, fist)—hang items on a line.

e. Tweezers—blunt end (fingers)—pick up small items such as rice and cereal bits.

f. Nutcracker (fist)—open nuts, turn small screw caps (this is a handy tool for opening bottle and jar lids).

g. Sugar or ice tongs (fingers)—pick up small items such as cotton balls and sort them into egg cups.

Wheels, Axles and Gears

- Put some blocks in a box. Push it across floor.
- Put rollers (dowels, round blocks, small logs, pencils) under the box and push it. It takes teamwork to keep transferring the rollers to the front edge of the box, but it's an easier way to move a heavy load.
- Make cookies using a rolling pin.
- Turn an eggbeater. Point out the gears. Notice how one gear turns the others. There are also gears inside a pencil sharpener.
- Wheel barrows use both wheels and levers to move loads.

Pulleys

Attach a rope line between two (clothesline) pulleys.

- Clip messages between two points using clothespins (levers).
- Hang a basket on the line and move loads.
- Rig a freight *elevator* with pulleys from a tree house or loft for lifting loads.
- Ski tows, fan belts, dentists' drills, cranes and radio dials all use pulleys. Make a pulley book by collecting pictures of pulley machines.

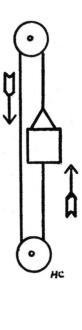

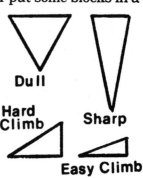

Inclined Plane and Wedge

Ramps, sloping roads, chisels, hatchets, plows, air hammers, carpenters planes—all of these are examples of the fourth basic machine: the inclined plane and its active twin brother, the wedge. The wedge includes all devices for cutting and piercing. When a wedge is sliced in half you get the inclined plane. The sharper the knife, the easier the cutting; the gentler the slope, the easier the climb.

- Construct a series of *ramps* at several pitches: a wide plank and some steps is an easy substitute. Take turns rolling a barrel up the various pitches or put some blocks in a box (or wagon) and pull it up the slopes. Ask: "Which slope is easier?"
- Chip wood with a chisel. Carve soap or banana with a knife.
- Trowel and shovel dirt.
- Use a needle. (A *jackhammer* is a very noisy wedge; a *needle*, a very quiet one.)
- Serve snacks. Bite and chew. Teeth are wedges!

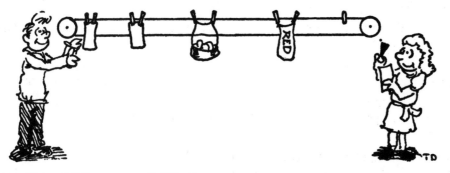

up ↑ 3 | *Screws*

The screw works in two ways, to raise weights and fasten objects.

- Use a screw jack to lift heavy objects. Examples of screw jacks are piano stools and screw type desk chairs.

- Turn a nut up and down on a bolt. Turn a screw into a board. Pound a nail (wedge) into the board. Try pulling both out with a claw hammer (lever). Which one could be pulled out more easily?

- Clamps and a bench vise use screws.

MUSIC—MOVEMENT

5 ↑ 3 | *I'm the Baby*

Ask children to imitate all the ways babies sound and move. Use the tape made at the Baby Party (see PEOPLE) to refer to sounds. The children may lie on their backs and wave their hands in the air, kick their feet, gurgle, burp, whimper, creep, crawl, roll over, cry, waddle,.

up ↑ 4 | *Building a Machine*

Use the following suggestions to build a machine with the group:

Form a circle and warm up, by moving various body parts, naming them and their motions (wiggle toe, swing arms).

Talk about machines, all kinds. Invite each child to think up a machine and demonstrate its motion, add sounds.

Make machine sounds, one at a time around the circle. Put all the sounds together. Use voice or body sounds. Add sounds made by various instruments.

Create one giant machine using the whole group, one at a time. Each child becomes a machine part and makes a motion attaching himself to the whole (physically touching another child).

"Workers" use "screwdrivers," "wrenches" and other tools to take the machine apart until it is all separated and its parts are sitting in the circle once again.

5 ↑ 3 | *This is What My Mommy (Daddy) Does*

(traditional, "Here We Go Round the Mulberry Bush")

Compose a song based on themes of parent occupations. Include work inside and outside the home. Example:

> *This is what my mommy does, mommy does, mommy does.*
>
> *My mommy goes to work, she does,*
>
> *Early Monday morning.*

5 ↑ 3 | *Bunny Wiggle*

Make gigantic pom-pom bunny tails by cutting magazine pages into strips up to the binding. Bend and staple the binding back to form a pom-pom. Attach a string so tail can be tied around waist. Add rabbit ears by taping ears to a cardboard headband. Do the bunny tail wiggle. Shake and hop to bunny-hop music. (See June— CREATIVE PROJECTS—*Pom Poms*)

Bunny Ear Headband

5↑3 Turtle Trot

- Children pretend to be turtles by crawling along the floor balancing "shells" on their backs. Shells can be made from flat cartons, sheets of cardboard, paper plates, etc.
- Crawl around the room trying to keep objects on back.
- Two children race with objects on back.
- Relay race. Child hands object from back to next contestant.

Read: *Tommy Turtle* from *Poems Children Will Sit Still For.*

5↑3 Turtle Games

- Decorate cartons with green paint and spots for turtle games and races.
- The children hide their eyes and are asked not to peek. One is sent out of the room and comes creeping back under a carton. Others guess "Who is the turtle?"

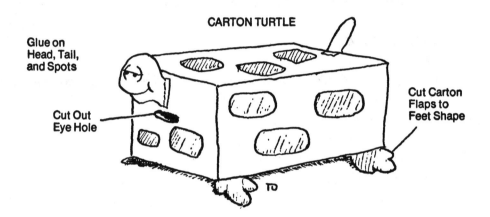

CARTON TURTLE

Glue on Head, Tail, and Spots

Cut Out Eye Hole

Cut Carton Flaps to Feet Shape

5↑3 Jackie Johnson Has a Motion

Substitute children's names to the tune of "Old MacDonald Has a Farm"

> *Jackie Johnson has a motion*
>
> *We can do it, too*
>
> *Jackie Johnson claps his hands*
>
> *And we can do it, too*
>
> *With a clap, clap here and a clap, clap there,*
>
> *Here a clap, there a clap, everywhere a clap, clap.*
>
> *Jackie Johnson claps his hands*
>
> *And we can do it, too.*

Continue with other verses

> *With a stamp, twist, shake, hop, spin, etc.*

5 ↑ 3 *Pussy Willow (Traditional)*

I know a little pussy, her coat is silver grey

She lives down in the meadow not so very far away

She'll always be a pussy, she'll never be a cat

'Cause she's a pussy willow, now what do you think of that?

Mew, mew, mew, mew, mew, mew, mew, mew, SCAT.

5 ↑ 3 *In the Spring (Tune: Sur le Pont d'Avignon)*

In the spring, in the spring,

Children playing, children playing,

In the spring, in the spring,

Children playing laugh and sing.

And they all do this way, Yes they all do that way.

In turn, each child chooses a motion for others to follow.

5 ↑ 3 *Eggs from the Inside*

Use plastic eggs.

Give one to each child. Ask them to feel, open, look inside the egg and think about how they might get out if they were tiny chicks growing inside. They might:

Tap inside with fingernails.

Make pecking noises with their mouths.

Roll up in a ball and pretend they are inside an egg.

Peck on the shell—break out all wet and bedraggled—shake dry.

Walk like tiny chicks—walk like a chick one week old, saying "peep."

Walk like a mother hen, clucking and calling her baby chicks, who come running.

On another day, become hatching baby ducks. Swim in a row behind the mother, bobbing heads down in the water with tails up.

LANGUAGE—DRAMA

5 ↑ 2 *Sibling Rivalry*

"I don't like baby!" Watch for signs of discontent, jealously, rivalry. Discuss problems directly. Be positive and understanding. Help the child think of ways to feel better through positive actions.

Problem	What to say
Does the baby keep Mommy very busy?	How can you help?
Do your toys get lost?	Can you keep them in higher places?
Do you miss sitting on Daddy's lap?	Ask him to hold you while baby is sleeping.

Dramatize situations. Talk about anger, hate, frustration. Share the comments and reactions of the children with parents.

Baby Cards

5 ↑ 3

When a baby arrives at the home of a child, the children in the center might make stories or poems and send cards. Use pictures cut from magazines and used baby cards as materials.

Occupations Alphabet

5 ↑ 3

Ask children to name occupations beginning with each letter of the alphabet. Draw or cut pictures to match and put together a book. Include children's names, relatives, friends, and neighbors to complete the alphabet.

> Henry's mom is an accountant.
>
> Robbie's aunt is a baker.
>
> Helen's dad is a contractor.
>
> Beverly's dad is a director.

Rhyming

5 ↑ 3

Make up one or two line verses to develop rhymes or read familiar poems leaving off rhyming words for the children to finish. Examples:

When I get into my bed,
I pull the covers over my _____

It is raining hard today
So we cannot go out to _____

I like to play, I like to sing
I like to do most _____

I got up very early today
Dressed myself neatly and went out to _____

The birds are singing, twee, twee, twee
I see their nest up in the_____

The rain is raining all around
It falls on the roof and it falls on the _____

Work Sequence

up ↑ 5

Use a series of pictures showing a particular job being carried to completion. For example, a shovel digging and filling a truck, the truck dumping the concrete, the stages of construction, the finished building. Lay them out on a table and ask children to arrange according to sequence. Ask contractors, vocational schools and factories for work photos. Also, advertising literature at building material centers.

Blarney (Multi-cultural)

up ↑ 3

- Enjoy a "Blarney Day" by using flattery and praise to excess. Exaggerate compliments, encourage the children to praise each other.

- Make up stories and dramatize situations using many words of flattery and praise. List the words.

Baby Mural

up ↑ 3

Construct a mural of baby faces cut from magazines. Talk about which baby has the sad face. Which is the plumpest? The thinnest? The happiest looking?

CREATIVE PROJECTS

Machine Constructions (On-going Projects)

up ↑ 5

Supply boxes, cartons, tubes, corrugated cardboard, wire, buttons, wheels, washers, tape, dowels, springs, plastic caps, etc.

- Divide children into groups of three or four, each to build a machine. Use several days or a week, allowing plenty of time for changes, additions, play, conversation and designing.

- When the machines are ready, have an inventors' meeting. Each team demonstrates and describes its machine. Encourage questions and new suggestions for other uses for the machines.

SCHOOL AGE

Weaving and Raveling

Provide a variety of weaving activities such as:

- Paper plate looms. Cut slits about 1" apart in the center of the plate. Weave in cardboard (stiff paper) strips, or strips of thin plastic cut from milk cartons.

- Construction paper looms. Weave with paper strips.

- Fence looms (chain link). Weave with canvas strips or plastic webbing.

- Pull apart woven fabrics such as canvas, coarse cottons, nylon, dish towels. Create fringes and use the pulled (crinkly) threads as hair for puppets and figures in drawings.

- Ravel knit items. Reuse the curly yarns in projects.

Bridge Construction—It Happened! (Following a pattern)

The purpose of this project was to determine how well the children (5's) could follow instructions to complete a pre-planned project. Each child was to build a bridge by pouring two concrete piers which would hold a road bed and two ramps.

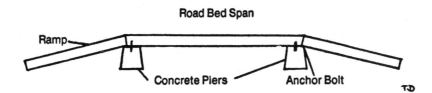

On the first day, the group held a meeting and the teacher described the plan which would be carried out over several days by a series of specific steps. First, each child built a *model* using unit blocks. They were asked to get specific sizes and numbers of blocks. They named the various parts of their models (piers, ramps, roadbeds).

On the second day, they mixed and poured concrete for the piers, using plastic bottles cut off as forms and setting in the anchor bolts. They held the bolts against the thickness of the boards to determine how high they should be set. The concrete was like "gush," "mud," "cakes." Next day, they were surprised to find how hard and heavy the forms had become.

On the third day, they built the ramps and bridge span by measuring and cutting lengths of 3" wide boards. Holes were drilled in the ends of the span and ramps, to fit over the anchor bolts. The ramps and span were painted black—"tarred."

On the fourth day, the teacher cut away the plastic bottle forms and the children assembled the bridges. White lines were painted on the roadbeds and the bridges were added to the block corner.

Toast Tweezer

Glue two tongue depressers together at one end with a 1/2" segment of dowel (1/2") in between. Decorate the sides with designs using acrylic paint. Use to lift hot toast from the toaster. Toast tweezers are a simple-to-make gift.

Rattles and Shakers

Make rattles and shakers from small plastic or metal containers such as squeeze lemons or band-aid boxes. Fill halfway with sand, rice, marbles, pebbles, beans, etc. Seal top to box with duct tape to be sure inside material doesn't spill.

- Analyze the sounds. Arrange from loud to soft. Develop a vocabulary for the different sounds of the shakers: "scratchy," "swishy," "rattly," "jingly," etc.

- Use in combination with other instruments to create sound effects for stories.

Plastic Squeeze Lemon...

...or Bandage Box

Paper Shakers and Streamers

- Cut a long fringe (6"–8") in strips of paper (newsprint, foil, tissue, construction, crêpe— for different sounds). Wrap the uncut end around paper tubes, straws and dowels. Shake, twirl between palms and blow into tubes to make different sounds—"rustles," "whishes," "crinkles," etc.

- Make 4'–6' streamers from crêpe paper. Attach to short (1') dowels/pencils. Swing and twirl into spirals, loops, wiggles, flutters. Attach streamers to fences and tree limbs. On a windy day, outside, watch the streamers and copy the many motions of the streamers. Inside, pretend the wind is blowing—against you, behind you, from the sides, whirling you around.

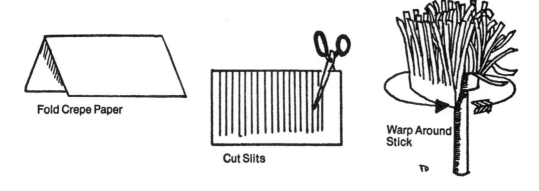

Fold Crepe Paper

Cut Slits

Warp Around Stick

JUST FOR FUN

5 ↑ 3 *Scarf Snatch*

One child sits in the middle of circle with eyes closed and a scarf on his/her head. Rest of group sit with hands behind their backs after choosing one to be "it.". "It" sneaks up and snatches scarf, hides it behind his/her back, then returns to the circle. The rest recite:

> *Such a cold and windy day*
>
> *Northwind blew your scarf away*
>
> *Tell us snowman if you know*
>
> *Where did Mr. Northwind go?*

Child in center tries to guess who is holding scarf.

up ↑ 4 *Turtle Puppet Games*

• Make turtles from felt or canvas. Fill with beans.

• Make turtles from mittens and socks. Stuff with cotton. Tie off toe and top to create head and tail. Attach felt feet.

• Lay out a trail or course of shapes. Use carpet squares, tape, chalk, cardboard pieces, etc. Make a spinner card with matching shapes. Child spins and advances a turtle to the shape shown by the spinner. Children take turns spinning and moving.

up ↑ 4 *Machine Games*

• Lay out an assortment of simple machines—egg beaters, clock, pencil sharpener, door knob, can opener, casters, faucet, scissors, knife, needle, hammer, wrench, etc.

Mark boxes with the labels of simple machines—lever, screw, axle, wedge, inclined plane, and pulley.

Sort the machines.

SCHOOL AGE

• Place the machines around the room. How many can children find?

• Look for machines in pictures (magazines, newspapers, books).

• Show machines and ask: "Who uses this machine?" "Name the job which uses this machine."

5 ↑ 2 *Chicken Hunt*

Buy or make tiny fuzzy yellow chick (cotton ball) to fit under or in a plastic egg. One child hides chick in one of several eggs in a basket. Other children try to guess where it is. The finder gets the next turn to hide the chick.

TODDLERS, TOO!

CURRICULUM takes into account the needs of developing children, but cannot be administered as medicine, forced on a sick patient. It can never remain constant, since life is always in motion.

SEQUENCE EIGHT

APRIL

APRIL THEMES

APRIL

Humpty Dumpty, A Foolish Egg

During April, spring continues to transform the landscape as *farmers plow* and *plant; baby birds hatch* from *eggs*, leave their *nests* and learn to fly. *Rain* nurtures and puts a shine on everything.

Children are also transformed! Look at their self-portraits and life-sized figures, drawn in September. Draw around the children again and hang the figures side by side—spring growth spurts show dramatic changes! The way each child completes the April *self-portrait* often shows much about manual dexterity, eye for detail and other observational skills. Comments about these portraits indicate how children feel about themselves.

Children "dressed" earlier figures with crayon and markers. These nude figures, made in April, might be dressed with wallpaper and cloth with fringed newspaper and raveled yarn for hair.

Water and its sources from tiny *streams* to huge *oceans* is vital to all life. *Floods* and *storms* cause water damage. *Plumbers* and *electricians* help to repair damage. *Dams, bridges, pipes, conduits, sewers, pumps* and *electricity* in *wires* help to control water and put it to work for us.

Fishermen and *sailors* work on *boats* on all kinds of *waterways* and at *docks, piers* and in *harbors*. *Farmers irrigate* with water to grow crops.

Rain uses all kinds of magic to create *mud, puddles, reflections, animal tracks—RAINY DAYS* are extra special.

"All by myself!" boast youngsters as they learn to *fold*—perhaps the diapers worn by the baby at home.

Science activities encourage children to experiment with water. What *floats* or *sinks*? Straws are *pumps*! Water can be moved and controlled with *funnels, troughs, gutters* and *buckets*.

We can create sounds with our bodies and be instruments in an "orchestra." *Cords* and *ropes* can be used to make shapes, letters, paths and stepping stones.

What would it be like to *build a nest* using only our "beaks" (mouths) as the birds do? With our motions we can develop fantastic dramas.

Nature creates all kinds of *flowers*. Children can use real *petals*, *tissue paper* and *egg shells*—to name just a few materials—to make fantasy flowers.

Following a *sensory walk* in the rain can you compose a *spring alphabet*? "A is for Ants, B is for Bees,...M is for Mud,...S is for Splash!,... V is for violets."

Did you know that *Humpty Dumpty* was an egg?

Don't forget to be silly and *April foolish*—JUST FOR FUN!

SEQUENCE EIGHT

PEOPLE

5
↑
4

Self Image—A New Look

Display a series of self image portraits of each child, done since they first came to the center. Talk about the differences, growth, changes, etc. Make new self portraits:

- Faces and silhouettes
- Full figures. Dress by painting or adding fabrics and yarn hair.
- Hand and foot prints.

up
↑
3

Plumbers/Electricians/Repair People

Help children understand what roles these people play.

Plumbers work mainly with pipes that carry water. They put in sinks, toilets, hot and cold water pipes.

Electricians work with the wires and cables that carry electricity for lights, TV, toasters, irons, electric stoves, etc.

Repair people fix things that are broken—from washing machines to chairs; cars to shoes.

All of these people are busy and are paid for their time. Ask a *retired* plumber or electrician to come talk about the work involved and possibly show the kinds of tools used.

up
↑
3

Fishermen/Sailors

- Show pictures of people at work on boats and docks.
- Show pictures of many kinds of boats—barges, tankers, tugs, liners, ferries, fishing trawlers, rowboats, pleasure craft, military vessels, research diving bells, etc.
- Set up play boats with cartons, block chairs, small tables (turned upside down with legs as masts). Supply oars, ropes, sails, cargo, fishing lines, nets.

EXPANDING OUR WORLD

up
↑
4

Plumbing

- Provide sections of pipe and hoses (6" to 2'), plastic, rubber, metal in various sizes (1/4" to 6"). Supply some "T"s, elbows, and other connectors. Children experiment, fitting pipes together, laying out lines.
- Tour the building, finding pipes and connectors to match the play pipes. Look for sewer pipes in the basement. Children in bathroom overhead tap floor and flush toilet so children in basement can hear the water run through the pipes.
- Follow a waterline from heater to tap. Feel the hot and cold pipes. Turn off under-sink shut-off valves. Show water main caps in the street. When maintenance workers dig and repair mains and sewers take children to see the pipes.
- Outside set up hoses and switches so children can experiment running water lines. (Remove the nozzles and keep water on low pressure.) Collect water at ends of lines to use on plants and for washing.

Bathroom Talk—It Happened!

"The toilet bowl is running over!"

The teacher ran for the plunger and discovered that a large wad of toilet paper was the cause of the flood. Several children came to watch the plumbing procedure. "I guess we need to have a meeting," commented the teacher. "Meetings" to discuss problems were a common event and the children arranged the seat blocks theater-style and gathered for the discussion.

When they were all settled, the teacher said in a very serious tone, "This meeting is to talk about what goes into the toilet."

With these four-year-olds, bathroom talk was prevalent, but always in a secretive manner. Now they were being *asked* to talk about such things. Their faces revealed their surprise. At first they were reluctant but once started they were *very* explicit. Their answers were accepted by the teacher and when they observed her serious expression their silliness subsided.

Then she gathered the group around her at a low table. "This is a plumbing experiment." "Experiment" was also a familiar word for they had often tested ideas by experimentation. On the table was a large glass bowl with a funnel set into a small glass so that it would stand upright inside the bowl, but the flow of water could be observed. First, the teacher ran water through the funnel. Then she took a wad of toilet paper and put it in the funnel. One of the children was asked to pour water into it. Only a trickle came through and as the water continued to pour in, the funnel filled and ran over the top. The children were quick to make the connection with what had happened to their toilet.

Following this experiment, another discussion was held about the proper use of toilet paper. They decided how many sheets were necessary and counted off four. As the roll of tissue was passed around, each child tore off four sheets.

Electricity

- Tour the building from electric entry lines (fuse box) and ask children to find where electricity is used. Show differences between phone and electric wires.

- Provide electric supply parts and sections of wire for children to study/touch. (Children cannot experiment with real switches and plugs due to dangers. Fives and up can do simple battery projects available in science texts.)

- Ask, "If you were an electrician, how many things in this room could you find to repair?" List and separate those requiring a special kind of repair service (i.e. telephone).

Appliance/Repair Shop

With advance permission, visit a repair shop. Ask owner to demonstrate a few simple tools, show the work bench and appliance being repaired. Ask: "What needed repair?" "Did you replace a part?" "Can we see the old and new part and where it goes on the appliance?"

Docks/Pier/Harbor/Waterway

Visit some area waterways and facilities. Look for the many kinds of jobs connected with water/docks/boats. Ask: "Is this water used for drinking? Pleasure? Transport?" "Is it a river, lake, reservoir, stream, ocean, etc.?"

SKILLS FOR DAILY LIVING

Folding

| 5 |
| ↑ |
| 3 |

- Practice folding skills using dish towels, doll blankets, small squares and rectangles of cloth.

- Practice folding with paper.

Wet Surfaces

| 5 |
| ↑ |
| 3 |

- Demonstrate how slippery wet surfaces can be. Let children feel the following items when dry: smooth wood, flat rock, a piece of metal such as used in slides. Pour water on and let them compare.

- Look outside and notice where people might slip—stone steps, wooden steps, ladder to the slide.

- Look at the bottoms of sneakers, shoes, rain boots. Which ones are least likely to slip?

CONCEPTS

Through/Around

| 5 |
| ↑ |
| 3 |

Show a short piece of pipe. Pour water or sand through it and say, "The water is going *through* the pipe." Lay the pipe in a pan of water and say, "Now the water is all *around* the pipe."

Colorless

| 5 |
| ↑ |
| 3 |

Show several colors, then hold up a glass of clear water. Ask, "What color is the water?"

Bring out the following ideas and new vocabulary. Water is *colorless*—no color. It is *transparent*—that means you can see through it. (What else is transparent? Glass, some paper, and plastic.) It is *translucent*—that means light shines through it.

Ovals

| 5 |
| ↑ |
| 3 |

One child said—"An oval is a circle that's been squeezed!"

Take both ends out of an empty soup can and sqeeze it in the center. Use as a pattern to make ovals. (If you squeeze one end more than the other you have an egg-shaped cookie cutter.)

SCIENCE

Eggs

| up |
| ↑ |
| 3 |

Serve eggs in a variety of ways over a several day/week period.

- Break and separate eggs into separate bowls. Cook the yolks (add a few whole eggs) into scrambles or bake into a custard.

- Whip and sweeten the whites, perhaps color with food color and serve as a meringue treat in a cone, or serve on top of custard or jello.

- Hard boil and cut with an egg slicer.

- Make egg nog/milk shakes.

- Use whole eggs in a cake mix.
- Make meringues/macaroons with whites.
- List all the foods children find in the cupboard (grocery shelf) which contain eggs.
- Serve eggs from white and brown shells. Can you taste any difference?

French Toast

Beat two large or three medium eggs in two cups of milk. Put in a shallow container such as a pie plate. Dip bread (dry bread is best) into the mixture, soaking both sides, then fry in hot, lightly buttered fry pan until golden brown. Serve with confectioner's sugar and jelly or syrup. If a little cinnamon and sugar is added to the egg mixture, no other topping will be needed. Cut in strips for children to eat as finger food.

Hands, Paws, and Tracking

Discuss the many uses of hands and paws. Compare the various ways different animals and birds make use of theirs. Ask about tails, fins, beaks, claws, etc.

- Experiment with holding and picking up items using just one finger, one finger on each hand, thumbs only, feet and toes.
- Walk to a muddy area beside a pond, in the woods or around animal pens to look for tracks.
- Use plaster of paris to make casts of tracks.
- Finger print children using an ink pad. At the police station they might also do this and tell how prints are used to find lost people. Show a birth certificate with a baby's foot or hand print.
- Follow a set of foot prints, animal or human.
- Lure small animals (squirrels, ducks) to a flat spot with bread or seeds. Put out shallow pans or puddles of non-toxic tempera paint. Observe and follow the track patterns.

Bees

- Show the pollen of flowers. Touch it with a Q-tip to demonstrate how it clings to an insect's legs.
- Sip honey water through a straw. Explain that flowers also contain nectar which the bees suck and carry to their hives to make honey to feed their babies. Pollen gets carried from flower to flower by birds and insects. This helps fruit and flowers grow.
- Read *Bees and Beelines* by Judy Hawes (pub. Thomas Crowell & Co.).
- Visit a field, flower garden, apiary or science center to watch bees at work.

Nesting Supplies

Hang bits of string, yarn, cotton batting on bushes and low limbs for birds to gather. Watch from inside the center to see what birds take the materials. If possible, watch to see where they go to build nests.

Nest Building

up ↑ 4

- Look for nests and watch for birds gathering nesting supplies.

- Gather grasses, needles, twigs, feathers. Mix with mud and shape into a nest. Dry. Line with feathers, leaves, cotton, soft grasses. Set in a tree in a secure, secluded place. Watch to see if birds will nest there.

   When the nest is ready, ask the children if they could make a nest as birds do, using beaks and claws.

Planting

up ↑ 3

- Plant—beans, carrots, cucumber, squash seeds, marigolds—all easily grown seeds. Count the number planted in each pot.

- Watch to see what happens. Did all seeds sprout? When did first leaves develop? If some did not, ask why? Were they watered every day? Did some tip over and need to be replanted? How tall were the seedlings after 5 days? 10 days? 2 weeks?

- Transplant outside when warm weather permits. If the seeds were started in peat pots, the whole pot can be put in the ground.

Soil Test

up ↑ 4

Discuss the idea that plants get nourishment (food) from the soil as people do from food. Fill one container with loam, the other with sand or gravel. Plant seeds or small plants in each. Do the same experiment in sunny and shady spots. Plant a small garden outside following the same procedure. Compare the growth of plants in both soils. Experiment by enriching soils with fertilizer.

Rain

up ↑ 4

Take advantage of rainy days. Talk about how they affect people—what they can and cannot do. When is rain fun, when is it a bother.? Read some descriptive poems and books about rain and draw pictures to illustrate them. Go outside and explore.

- Look for spider webs, plants, rock crevices where water collects in drops and puddles.

- Find reflections. Drop pebbles into puddles to create rings. Watch changes in reflections as the water ripples.

- Look for drip marks under eaves and erosion trenches where soil washes away.

- Listen to rain falling on different surfaces—foil, cardboard, empty cans and cartons, glass, cars, or into containers of water. List the words children use to describe the sounds.

- Ask, where does rain come from? Read *You and the World Around You* by Selsam (pub. Doubleday).

Waterproofing

5 ↑ 3

Read about waterproofing in the book *The Chinese Knew* by J. Levine and T. Pine (pub. McGraw-Hill). Why do we wear raincoats? Stretch a handkerchief over a glass. Pour water over it slowly. Do this with an old sweater, piece of plastic, rubber, canvas. Does the water go through some things faster than others?

Gutters

up ↑ 5

- Watch gutter activity around the playground and neighborhood. What kinds of things are carried and caught by storm sewers and culverts? Build a simple tunnel by burying a large 3'5" section of downspout or drain pipe under the sand. Pour water and float things through the tunnel.

- Build sections of trough by nailing three boards together. Line with plastic. Run troughs between containers, down slopes, and across the yard. Pour water into high end. Follow the water by floating objects—ping pong balls, leaves, crumpled paper— along the water course. Time the flow with a stop watch. Race objects by timing them.

Pumps

up ↑ 4

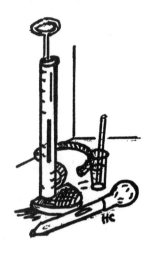

- Supply pumps such as basters and straws for water play.
- Use a small aquarium pump and hoses at a water table.
- Show children the washing machine when water is pumping out.
- Pump air into an inner tube with a tire pump.
- Attach a vacuum cleaner hose at the exhaust end to pump air into a large plastic bag.
- Inflate an air mattress with a foot pump.
- Demonstrate a blood pressure instrument using the syringe.

Float or Sink

up ↑ 3

- Place objects of various kinds (crayons, cork, nail, plastics, string, rock) beside the water table. Provide two sorting trays marked "FLOATS" and "SINKS"! Children sort objects.

- Make simple boats by attaching paper sails to a variety of flat objects of paper, wood, plastic, metal. Children float the boats. Which worked? Why? How long?

- Sort pictures of floaters and sinkers into sets. Make into books.

Displacement

up ↑ 5

Float a large plastic container in water table or sink. Fill to limit with variety of objects— stones, nails, sand, shells, foam—one specific item each time. Mark the sides to show amount of water displaced by each loading. Observe the sides of the "vessel" as it is loaded. What happens? Show pictures of large ships with displacement marks painted on the sides.

Sunken Ship

up ↑ 4

Put an empty bottle into water. It floats. Tip it slightly so water begins to go in. What happens? To demonstrate how sunken ships can be raised, put a tube or hose down into the bottle and blow air into it. As water is displaced with air, the bottle will come to the surface.

Sensory Hunt

up ↑ 4

Divide into four groups. Go outside separately with four different assignments. Smelling group—Listening group—Touching group—Looking group. Take each to the same areas to explore with their special sense. Compare, list, discuss what each group discovered.

Patterns and Sequences

5 ↑ 3

Cut a variety of shapes from assorted colors of construction scraps. One child chooses ten (or less) and arranges them in a pattern on floor or table. Other children then choose from the collection and assemble a matching sequence of colors and shapes.

MUSIC—MOVEMENT

up ↑ 4 *Leg and Foot Work*

- How many ways can you use your legs? What occupations rely on legs? How many different ways can you walk? In what different ways do animals use their legs?

- Put corks on floor. Remove shoes and stockings and try to pick up with toes.

- Mime the following motions. Walk under a low bridge. Walk through mud, puddles, jump across a brook, climb a slippery hill, fall down, get mud all over your hands and arms, wash it off. Walk in big boots, slippers, heels, etc.

up ↑ 4 *Cords and Ropes*

- Using six foot (approx.) sections of cord or rope, make into circles on the floor. Walk around inside, outside. Sit in your own little circle. Put cords on the floor in line and walk as if on a tightrope. Step one foot after another, heel and toe. Sideways. On toes. Or heels. Hop back and forth over the line. Accompany motions with drumbeats.

- Make cords into numbers, letters, shapes and patterns. Look at a shape then pick it up and ask who can walk the same shape.

- Draw a pattern on paper or blackboard and ask children to copy on the floor using cords.

up ↑ 4 *Body Orchestra*

Use bodies, motion, sounds to create instruments. Orchestrate the rhythms and sounds.

Leader talks to the group with instructions such as:

Snap fingers.

Pound chests with clenched fists.

Stamp feet.

Tap fingernails on floor.

Rap knuckles on floor.

Slap flat of one hand and then two hands on floor.

Rub flat of hand on a hard surface making circular movement.

Shuffle feet.

Mouth sounds: whistle, hum, kiss, click tongue, siren, swish, inhale and exhale. Say, "Oooo or ahhh," be excited, happy, angry, sad or scared.

- Ask: "Can you think of another way?"

- Build a sound up to loud and take it back to soft.

- After experimenting with sounds, divide the group and 'play' two different sounds at once, teacher acting as the conductor. As group learns to follow the conductor, continue dividing into 3, 4, 5, 6...sections.

- Combine sound sections with a story, each one contributing its own effect, sometimes two or three at once, sometimes entire "orchestra."

- Experiment with dynamics, staccato, legato, fast (vivaci), slow (largo), to introduce real music terms. (SCHOOL AGE)

5 ↑ 3 *Rain Dance*
Children close their eyes. Ask: What would it feel like to be a raindrop? Lots of little soft pattering drops? Show this with fingers. Now it is raining hard. It is thundering, beat on drums. The rain is coming harder and harder, the wind is blowing, and now the storm is over.

5 ↑ 3 *Rhino Ripple*
Read *Rhinoceros Skin* from Kipling's *Just So Stories*. Say: "Make yourself very, very tight. *Tight, tight*, squeeze! Now let go! *Loose, loose*, flappy and flabby!"

LANGUAGE—DRAMA

up ↑ 5 *Alphabets Around Themes*
Develop alphabets around themes, such as seasons, occupations, foods, rooms, (kitchen). Example:

Spring Alphabet by Cléa Chmela

A is for Ants

B is for Butterflies and Bees

C is for Caterpillars

D is for Dandelions

E is for Eggs

F is for Flowers and Frogs

G is for Gardens

H is for Hives and Honey

I is for Insects and Itch

J is for Jumping Frogs

K is for Kites

L is for Lions and Lambs

M is for Meadows and Mice

N is for Nests

O is for Outdoors

P is for Puddles and Pansies

Q is for Quacking

R is for Rain

S is for Sprinkles and Spiders

T is for Tadpoles

U is for Umbrellas

V is for Violets

W is for Wind

X is for eXercise

Y is for Yellow-Forsythia, Sun

Z is for BuzzzzzzZZZZZZZ

5 ↑ 3 *Humpty Dumpty*
Read the poem and dramatize the actions. Encourage children to recite the rhyme as they act the drama. Do they realize Humpty Dumpty was an egg?

up ↑ 4 *Children's Story Time*
When the children in the group are familiar with the classroom library books, set aside a special time each day when one or two children may choose a favorite book and 'read' it to the class. Some may bring books from home. Keep a record of who has had a turn but assure the children that this is strictly voluntary.

April

Rain Poem

Have You Ever Walked in the Rain?

by Helen Campbell

Have you ever walked in the rain?
I have...
The raindrops beating on my hat,
My boots sloshing through a puddle
And the wet, wet feeling on my face.
Have you ever walked in the rain?
I have...

Have you ever walked in the fog?
I have...
It closes in softly about you
And makes you open your eyes wide
To peer into nothing.
Have you ever walked in the fog?
I have...

Have you ever run in the wind?
I have...
The rush of noise about your ears,
Hair whipping your head,
The feel of fresh air warming your skin,
Have you ever run in the wind?
I have...

CREATIVE PROJECTS

Rain Painting

- Put some globs of finger paint on a sheet of paper or sprinkle dry poster paint on paper and hold it under the rain to create designs.

- Chalk or paint on pavement and watch the rain's effect.

- Easel paint in a light drizzle.

- Drop dry paint into egg cups in one, two, three color mixes. Set in the rain.

- Lay leaves, plastic shapes, a glove, or coins on sheets of colored construction paper. Put under light rain for a *short* time. Remove the objects to reveal dry patterns. Do the same activity on a sunny day. Leave the papers for several days until the color fades. Cover sheets with plastic to protect from moisture.

- Make letters and shapes on paper with masking tape and repeat the above experiment, removing the tape to reveal the letters and shapes.

Tissue Paper Flower Raindrops

Put tissue paper petals in flower designs between raindrop-shaped wax papers. Hold in place with small dabs of paste. Press, waxed sides together, with a warm iron (under brown paper). Punch a hole for hanging strings and hang into mobiles.

Tinsel Rain

Use foil and plastic holiday tinsel to make rain pictures. Hang them in shadow box panoramas to make rain effects.

Egg Shell Pictures

Save and dry cracked egg shells. Fill small bowls about half full of water and add food colors. Stir in crushed shells until color adheres, strain and dry on paper towels. Paint thinned glue onto construction paper in free form designs, or paint glue over pre-drawn pictures and sprinkle with colored eggshells. Shake mixed colors of shell bits onto glue to create mosaic pictures.

Giant Eggs

Children mix pastel shades, using white with the tempera paints. Cut big egg shapes from cardboard (about 8"-10" long). Paint the shapes with the pastels. When dry, decorate with scraps of lace or trim, or use construction scraps and pinking shears to cut paper trims, or use dry markers and make zig-zags, swirls, ripples, etc.

Onion Bags

- Cut onion bag open and stretch over nails on a frame to use as a weaving base. Use blunt needles or a bobby pin to weave with yarn.
- Make crayon rubbings through paper laid over an onion bag.

Birds

Crumple tissue paper into balls. Wrap with pipe cleaners, forming birds' feet with wire ends. Add wings and beak of construction paper. Hang with strings or secure with wire feet to twigs.

Picture Puppets

Mount pictures of animals on cardboard and attach holding sticks (tongue depressors). Children choose a picture puppet and imitate the sound of the animal or choose an instrument which best imitates the sound. Make stories to go with the puppets and fit them together. When telling or reading stories about animals, ask if there is a puppet to go along with the story and appoint children to hold them up at the appropriate times in the story.

Paper Making

- Chop in a food processor to a fine pulp: peanut shells, dry leaves, some newspaper scraps and *fine* wood chips or sawdust.
- Mix with water to a thick, *pulpy* mash in a large tub or water table.
- Spread and strain the pulp through fine screening. Lay on a cloth, cover with a cloth and roll the pulp flat with bottles or rolling pins. Air dry for a few hours.
- Iron the pulp, *through the cloth*, until dry. Carefully lift off the coarse sheet of paper.
- Read *The Chinese Knew* by J. Levine and T. Pine, McGraw-Hill.

SCHOOL AGE

Flowers

- Foot flowers. Children take off their shoes and stockings and trace around their own or each others' feet. Paint and cut out. Add stems and leaves. Or, step in pans of paint and print flowers.

- Rub colors from flower petals to color shapes drawn on white paper.

- Paint thinned glue onto petal shapes and fill with real petals.

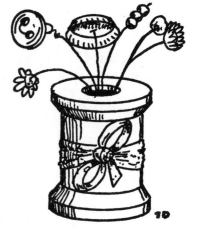

- Cut from pictures or draw flowers. Attach to pipe cleaners, telephone wire or sticks. Put into spools, or paper cups turned upside down with holes punched for the stems.

- Cut petal *shapes* from colorful magazine pages. Paste into flowers on individual or large mural paper.

- Trace petal shapes in wet sand. Fill with dandelions and other wild flowers.

- Trace around real petals and leaves to make designs.

Egg Blowing

- Puncture a small hole in both ends of raw eggs with a needle. Insert a cake tester or long needle to pierce the yoke for easier blowing.

- Hold egg over dish and blow contents.

- Rinse several times with water. Dry.

- Set in small juice cups or egg trays to paint. Dry first coat and add designs.

- Run a hanging thread through using a long darning needle. Tie a button or bead at bottom and a hanging loop at the top.

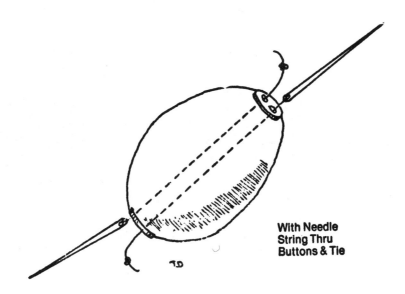

**With Needle
String Thru
Buttons & Tie**

__JUST FOR FUN__

Foolish Skits

- Rearrange familiar plots from rhymes and stories (The Three Bears, Little Miss Muffet, etc.). Tell them backwards or mix up two different stories or rhymes.
- Dramatize nursery rhymes and group guesses which one.
- One child chases another with water bucket. Finally throws water at audience. Confetti has been substituted.
- Adults dress in ridiculous costumes on April Fools' Day. Bathing suits; wear winter hats and mittens; put boots on the wrong feet; wear a bathrobe over clothing.

Dandelion/Daisy Relay

Divide into teams of 3 to 6 each. Child from each team runs to pick a flower and brings it to the next child. Flower is put in a cup of water. That child runs to pick a flower, etc. Flowers must have stems long enough to stand in the cup. The team which has picked all its flowers first wins the relay.

- Vary the game with different motions to get to the flowers—hopping, crawling, rolling, etc.
- Pick only the flower heads and lay around or fill the outlines of a flower on the ground. Race to see which team can complete its flower first.

Egg Scotch

Make two sets of egg-shaped markers in various colors and patterns from wallpaper samples. Lay out one set in a meandering path. Children draw from the matching set, follow the path to find the matching egg.

Boats

Sailboat

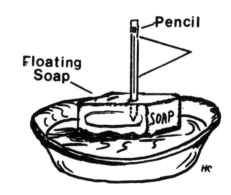

Shoe Box Ship

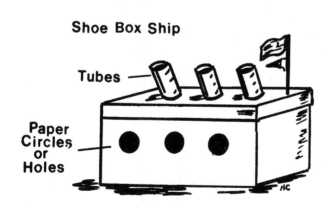

LEAVE the doors of your mind open to new ideas—never let your convictions become encased in cement. Let your "I AM" develop to the point where you can experiment with enthusiasm, succeed with satisfaction, and fall flat on your face without frustration or a sense of overwhelming failure.

SEQUENCE NINE

MAY

MAY THEMES

MAY

Cocoons, Kites and Kimonos

During May, the people theme focuses on the many **Asian cultures** which enrich the palette (and palate) of American life. We might make tasty **rice** dishes, sample **tofu, almond float** or **orange pudding**. Children can transform turtle cartons used in April into **dragons** to breathe fire in a dance. **Kites** and **toss-cups, sun hats** and **kimonos**, and oriental-sounding music played on the black piano keys adds atmosphere to a celebration in the style of **Chinese New Year**.

Concepts about **growing things** inside and outside can be enriched by visits to **farms, nurseries, dairies** and other **food sources**. We help children to understand the food chain by tracing its route from **farms** and **supermarkets** to tables and lunch boxes. Geographical areas each have a particular job to fill in the **food supply**. **Fishing fleets, canneries, orchards, vegetable and berry farms, poultry and egg producers, cattle ranches, dairies and bakeries—ice cream stands!**—help to provide nourishment. What kinds of foods are produced where you live?

As children discover the many forms of **food production**, they enrich their understanding about how people help people. They witness how people **care for, feed** and **protect plants and animals**, just as their parents feed and protect them. Such ideas add special meaning as they think about **mothers,** the very first people to nurse and protect them.

Dairy products as common as milk and cheese or as exotic (to some) as **yogurt** play an important part in our nutrition. Have you ever had **tofu**, a soy milk product?

Farm animals of all kinds, especially cows, are important friends in our food chain.

Caterpillars to cocoons, seeds to seedlings, frog eggs to tadpoles, each process teaches us something about life cycles.

Experiments with **salt** and **evaporation, vibrations, seriation** and **butter making** are suggested in May science activities.

How do **colors** make us **feel**? Can we "dance" a color? **Imaginary friends** and **make-believe**; **May baskets** and **May poles**; fanciful **insects** and **butterflies**—all these things help turn May time into a perfectly **pink** and **purple** passion (to emphasize just one of the 21 consonants).

JUST FOR FUN—fly a **fish kite** and top off merry May with a **May box picnic** on **Boy-Girl Day!**

SEQUENCE NINE

PEOPLE

Food Producers, Growers

- Food comes to us from farms, dairies, ranches, orchards, fisheries, apiaries, etc.

- Talk about a dairy farm, a poultry farm, a truck farm, a wheat farm and a cattle ranch. How are they different? What does each provide?

- How does a farmer's life compare to that of a banker, a teacher, a mechanic, a bus driver? (Hours they work, kinds of things they do, clothes they wear.)

- Look for pictures to post and read stories about people who produce food.

- Ask: How does food get to the table? Follow the various routes and carriers from the source. Use dramatic play with specific foods such as apples, milk, eggs, cereal, etc.

Food Servers

- Waiters, waitresses, cooks, vendors, etc. The children can do all of these jobs. Practice taking orders, serving and clearing tables. How many items can you remember? Which person ordered the food? What do you say when the food is not as you ordered it?

- Make books using pictures and ideas from each of these first two activities.

Mothers

- Mothers often perform all of the above jobs. Ask each child to name the many ways his/her mother provides food. Some may be nursing mothers.

- Make "My Mother's Jobs" books by looking through picture books, magazines, newspapers. Children point to the picture—"My mother can do that!" Write down the activity or cut out the picture.

- Make a large mural showing all the jobs done by the mothers of the children. When mothers come to the center ask each one to point to jobs she does at home and at work. Ask mothers to write words or bring pictures of jobs not shown in books or the mural. After a mother points to her jobs, applaud and cheer.

EXPANDING OUR WORLD

Farm/Supermarket

- Visit a farm at planting, growing or harvesting season. Talk in advance about what the children might expect to see. If possible, go to the same farm in different seasons.

- Ask the farmer about the things to be done in a day. An adult takes notes so the various tasks can be made into job cards later.

- If no farm is within reach, visit a supermarket. Match different foods to their source, i.e. milk from a dairy farm, eggs from a poultry farm, vegetables from a truck farm, etc.

- Ask the manager how the different foods got to the store.

Asians (Multi-cultural)

up ↑ 4

- Display books, records, toys, dolls, food containers, art objects, costumes, fans, baskets, calendars, travel folders and post cards, bamboo items, chop sticks—any item which comes from an Asian culture.

- List the many Asian countries. Post a map with yarn lines from names to country represented. Put heart stickers and names of children from these countries beside the map.

- Use the Discovery Table (see September) to set up a display of items from homes of Asian families in the group.

- Play a record or listen to Asian languages spoken by parents and staff members. Teach children a few words—greetings, foods, activities, clothing, etc.

- How would you travel to these countries? How did families at the center come to America?

Chinese Restaurant/Gift Shop (Multi-cultural)

up ↑ 4

- Arrange with the owner of a restaurant to visit at a time before opening to see how foods are prepared, i.e. wontons, noodles, fortune cookies.

- Ask the owner to write each child's name in Asian language characters.

- Buy samples of food to take back to the center.

- Visit a gift shop where Asian products are on display.

SKILLS FOR DAILY LIVING

Reasoning

up ↑ 4

To determine a child's intellectual growth, play the following games:

- REPEATING A SERIES: Start with two numbers or words (colors, objects, animals) and add one at a time. "I went to the store and I bought..." Child takes turn with teacher in adding item.

- STRETCHING IMAGINATION: "Would you find an elephant in the bathtub?" "Why not?" "The airplane stopped at a red light." Make up a story, one child starts and each child adds a part.

- MEMORY CONCENTRATION: Place articles on table. Rearrange or take one away while child is not looking. "What is missing? Or different?"

- PROBLEM SOLVING: Pose a problem, such as "If you were lost what would you do?" "If the person taking care of you fell down and couldn't get up or talk to you, what would you do?"

- FOLLOWING DIRECTIONS: Show a model of an object or picture and the step-by-step instructions, using pictures and words, for making a copy. Can the child follow the directions and make the object?

- RECOGNIZING PROPERTIES: Show a familiar object. How much can a child tell about it—color, size, weight, use, smell, etc.?

- OBSERVATION—DISCRIMINATION: Use a series of objects to explore likenesses and differences. How many does the child see? Color? Shape? Size? Use?

- CATEGORIZING: Show a series of pictures or objects. Ask: Which do not belong? For example: orange, baby, bread, egg.

up
↑
3

Greetings (Verbal and Social Skills, Multi-cultural)

- Ask: "How many ways can we greet other people?" (Smiles and nods, hand shakes, verbal greetings, hugs and kisses.)

- Practice some of the ways suggested by the children. Teach some foreign words, especially from languages of children of other cultures in the group.

- In many Asian countries, people habitually greet each other by folding their hands in front of them in prayer form and bowing slightly.

5
↑
4

Naps (Siesta Time)

When children get to four and five they are apt to resist taking naps. Try shifting the emphasis.

- Show picture of a man leaning against a tree, large hat over his face. Say: "He is taking a *siesta*—another word for a nap. In southern countries like Mexico, almost everyone naps in the early afternoon when the sun is very hot."

- Find a picture of a sleeping cat. "How many of you have a cat? Have you noticed how often they curl up and go to sleep? Their bodies know they need to rest so they will have energy to run and play."

CONCEPTS

up
↑
5

Perspective

- Look at landscape pictures. Ask: "Which objects (trees, houses, people) are farther away? How do you know they are? Draw three trees (triangles or circles with trunks). Draw one near, one a little farther away and one in the distance."

- Show a picture of a highway or tracks. Ask: "Which end of the road or tracks is farther away? Look at a long hallway or down a long sidewalk. Do they seem to grow narrow at the far end? Measure the width where you are. Measure the width a distance away. Compare the results."

- Lay a 10' or 12' piece of board on the ground. Look down its length. Repeat the measuring experiment.

up
↑
4

Purple Mixing

- Mix red, blue, white paints to create shades of purple.

- Sing the song "Lavender's Blue" and change the color and rhyming words as colors appear, i.e. "Lavender's fuchsia, willy, willy...lavender's pink, frilly, frilly...lavender's purple, silly, silly," etc.

up
↑
4

Flower Colors

Collect real or seed catalog pictures of flowers. Match with paint shades created in the activity above.

up
↑
4

Purple Paper Mural

Cut, tear and collect paper scraps of various purples from print materials (magazines, catalogs, advertising fliers). Use to fill the design sections of a mural (flowers, grapes, etc.).

Shape Games (Sets/Seriation)

Cut construction paper/cardboard into strips of various lengths, shapes of several sizes each.

- Arrange by length, color, shape, size, etc.
- Cut or fold circles into fractions (pie shapes). Ask children to put together to make whole, halves, quarters, thirds.
- Lay large shapes on the floor. Divide into teams to find objects of the same shape.
- Put assorted shapes into piles of matching sets. Children form relay teams. First player chooses a shape from one pile, finds the match, lays shapes in pairs. Next child takes a turn. First team to match all sets wins.

SCIENCE

Dairy Products

- Name foods which contain milk or are made from milk.
- Each day, serve samples of dairy products.
- Cook using dairy products. Some suggestions for children to make:
    - Cream sauce with meat or vegetable bits, served on toast
    - Puddings
    - Cheese sauces or melts

Butter Making

Experiment with three ways, using three half pints of heavy cream. Children in three groups take turns:

- Shaking cream in a covered jar.
- Beating cream with a hand beater.
- Beating cream with an electric beater.

Yogurt

Make yogurt. Heat milk to 120°, do not boil. Cool. Stir in a tablespoon of plain yogurt (starter). Cover and stand in a warm place for 6-8 hours or over night until solid and creamy. Store in refrigerator. Flavors can be added to the cooled milk—vanilla, honey or sugar.

Rice (Multi-cultural)

In many Asian cultures, rice is the major food in the diet. How and where is it grown?

- Cook boiled rice and serve in several different ways—with butter; brown sugar and cinnamon; tomato sauce; soy sauce; sprouts; meat bits.
- Taste rice cakes, compare with rice cereals.
- Sprout and plant rice kernels.
- Compare brown rice, white rice and wild rice.

Tofu (Multi-cultural)

Invite an Asian cook, grocery merchant or restaurant owner to demonstrate how tofu is made. Compare the process with making yogurt, above. Serve cubes of tofu in a clear meat or vegetable broth.

Almond Float (Hsing-Jen-To-Fu) (Multi-cultural)

2 pkg. unflavored gelatin		Syrup:	2 cups water
1 3/4 cup cold water			1/2 cup sugar
1 1/2 cups cold milk		Garnish:	6 1/2 oz. can
1 tbsp. almond extract			Mandarin oranges
			1 lb. can litchi nuts

This is a modern version of a classic Chinese dish. The original recipe did not use almond extract or gelatin. The jelling agent in the original was agar-agar, a type of seaweed, boiled until it dissolved, producing a clear, flavorless aspic. Because agar-agar produces jellies of varying consistencies, it is difficult to use with any precision. Instead of almond extract, the ancient Chinese crushed whole almonds, soaked them in water and squeezed out the liquid.

a.   In pyrex bowl, sprinkle gelatin over 1/2 c. cold water, soften 5 minutes.

b.   Bring 1 1/4 c. water to boil and add to gelatin. Stir until dissolved and clear, add milk and extract. Pour mixture into flat 7 1/2 x 12 dish. (Custard should be about 1 1/2 inches thick, 3 to 4 hours in refrigerator until set).

c.   Make syrup with sugar and water. Boil and chill—it will be thin.

d.   Assemble: Cut custard into diagonal slices, then diamond servings. Serve on plate. Garnish with oranges and nuts—pour syrup over all.

Orange Pudding (Hsi-Mi-Cho-Ken) (Multi-cultural)

1/2 cup pearl tapioca	2 1/2 cups cold water
1 large orange	1/4 cup sugar

Prepare ahead: In a small bowl cover tapioca with 1/2 c. cold water, soak 4 hours. Peel orange, remove membranes, break into small pieces.

To cook: In 2 quart pan, combine 2 1/2 cups water with sugar. Bring to boil, stir until sugar dissolves. Pour tapioca (drained) in pan slowly, stirring constantly. Cook two minutes, until thick. Add orange, re-boil. Serve hot.

Cows/Cattle (Multi-cultural)

In many tribal cultures, especially African, cattle are counted as we count money. They are traded for land and given as wedding gifts.

Most cultures raise, tend and herd this common animal and use milk, dairy products and meat provided by cattle.

Have the children seen and heard a real cow? Can you provide such an experience?

Use mural paper to make a life-sized cow. Paint "Bossy" brown and black, glue on white spots. Hang a rubber glove (udder bag) underneath, fill with water, and show how cows give milk.

Farm Animals

*   Find pictures of farm animals and paste on a chart.

*   Name the various uses beside each animal, i.e. work, pleasure, foods, products, etc.

*   Compare animals to machines which do the same work, i.e. horse—plow.

*   Visit a farm to observe live animals and/or show films of live animals.

up ↑ 3 *Capturing Small Pets*

When classroom animals (hamsters, gerbils, etc.) escape from cages:

Place plastic buckets or waste baskets (smooth sided) in various areas around the building, near kitchens or pantries. Construct a stairway up the sides of the tubs, using blocks, or make ramps up to the rim using screening. Place some food and nesting material in the buckets.

Rub carrots or crumbs on the ramp or stairway to leave food scents.

Leave a trail of food scraps leading to the traps. Check the traps each morning. Hamsters, gerbils and mice are nocturnal and will probably hunt for food during the night.

up ↑ 3 *Frog Eggs*

Collect "slow" water, including some algae (green scum) from a pond where frogs hatch. Put in a large glass container or aquarium. Add pond water and algae every four or five days. Make a rock and mud pile on the bottom.

Collect frog eggs in their jelly mass.

When eggs hatch and tadpoles are formed, feed with water beetles or commercial fish flakes.

Release tadpoles back into the same pond when well formed.

up ↑ 3 *Seed Growth*

Use two pieces of glass (approx. 4"x6"). Cut paper towel to same size. Make a wire holder as shown in sketch. Lay towel on one glass. Sprinkle seeds on towel. Lay on second piece of glass. Tape or hold together by elastics. Place in wire rack. Set in shallow pan of water. Water will seep through towel (capillary action) and seeds will sprout. Keep moist. (Grass seeds grow quickly.)

Glass Plates — Paper Towel — Wire Rack — Seedling — Tray of Water

up ↑ 4 *Winged Seeds*

- Collect winged maple seeds. Remove dry husks to reveal the seeds. Plant some.
- Drop winged seeds from a high place or toss them in the wind. Ask: "Why does the seed need wings?"
- Look for seedlings and saplings of various sizes around a mature maple. Transplant some in pots. *Hug* the big tree!
- Show maple wood products i.e. cutting board, bowl, etc.
- Glue winged seeds to paper and add lines to create designs and winged creatures.

Salt

Discover the properties and uses of salt, a mineral deposited by the oceans long ago. Bodies need salt. Chlorine comes from salt. Chlorine is used to purify water. Salt is used in making soap.

- Smell and taste salt. Taste some water. Dissolve salt in water until it disappears. Taste the salt water.

- Taste salted and unsalted vegetables. Taste foods seasoned with salt and salt substitutes.

- Mix 2 teaspoons salt in a pint of water. Put in the freezer until 1/4" ice layer has formed. Remove ice, rinse and taste. Can you taste the salt?

 ### Evaporation

- Repeat the last experiment above. When the ice forms, separate and boil. Boil the unfrozen water. When the two have boiled away (evaporated), which pan has a residue of salt? Ask: How do you think we could get drinking water from the ocean in the winter? (Eskimos)

- Evaporate salted water in a shallow pan in the sun. Taste the salt residue. Ask: How could we get salt from the ocean?

- Boil a tablespoon of salt in a quart of water for ten minutes. Remove some and cool. Boil the remainder for ten minutes, cool. Taste both. Which is saltier?

 ### Melting with Salt

Drop salt on an ice cube. What happens? Why are icy roads salted?

Measure the temperature of salted and unsalted water. What is the difference?

 ### Rock Salt Crystals

Put loam in a small metal pan or jar lid. Stir salt into a glass of water until it no longer dissolves easily—a few grains still appear at the bottom. Pour some salt water on the soil to make mud. Lay a loop of copper wire on the mud. (Remove coating from copper telephone wire.)

Dry mud in the sun or warm place. Look for salt crystals on the wire and in the dried mud.

 ### Vibrations/Telephones

Demonstrate how sound travels through objects:

- Pluck rubber bands, guitar strings, a long cord stretched tightly between two points.

- Put funnels in the two ends of a hose—a speaker and an ear piece. This is for *whispering* only, no loud sounds which could damage ear drums. (4's, 5's and up)

- Try whisper experiments with and without the *Whisper Phone* (above).

- Make a telephone with two tin cans and a string.

- Place hand over larynx and hum.

- Tap a tuning fork. Match the pitch on a piano or an instrument string.

- Hold a ruler on the edge of a table with 5" extending beyond the edge. Bend to vibrate.

- Hold a yardstick to the ear and place a clock at the other end. Repeat using a metal curtain rod.

- Hold one end of a pencil or small piece of dowel between the teeth and scratch on the other end.

up ↑ 4 *Rice Rattles (Sensory)*

Provide a collection of covered containers (cardboard, plastic, metal, paper, glass, cloth (bags), etc.) Put some rice in each one, shake and observe the difference in sounds. Make a set of graduated sounds—loud to soft.

MUSIC—MOVEMENT

5 ↑ 3 *Kites*

Make the motions of flying a kite: run to launch; unwind the line; tug the line; pull and run with the kite; hold the line tightly, tugging it as the kite dips, spins, dives and soars. Reel it in.

Be the kite: whirl, dip, dive, flutter, soar, spin, go limp, crash.

5 ↑ 3 *Farm Play*

- Put pictures or puppets of farm animals, one at a time, into a "barn" (carton). Children take turns —"letting the cow (etc.) out to exercise and feed." Another child tells by the motions which animal is in the pasture. Children guess by making the sounds of each animal.

- Sing a verse of "Old MacDonald" (substitute child's name) after each animal is named. Sing verses all together as teacher points to children holding the animal picture, filling in the animal names.

up ↑ 4 *Dragons (Multi-cultural)*

- Make dragons from cartons as suggested by the illustration. Cut arm and head holes in sides and top.

- Hitch dragon parts together with ropes along the side. Dancers hold the ropes.

- Dragons are trimmed with rattlers, shakers, streamers, pom poms and bells. In China, such noise makers are used to keep birds and insects from gardens.

- Make individual carton dragons, each with a head and a long tail.

- Combine the DRAGONS with the next activity.

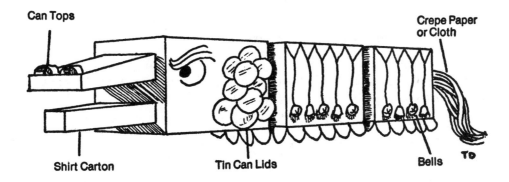

Can Tops   Crepe Paper or Cloth

Shirt Carton   Tin Can Lids   Bells   TO

up ↑ 4 *Oriental Music*

Make music which sounds oriental by playing only on the black keys on a piano. Add gong, bells and drums. Make up names for songs based on oriental themes—The Dance of Fu Lee's Cricket, Kimono Waltz, Rice Harvest Motions, etc.

Netting

5 ↑ 3

Give children pieces of netting in a variety of colors. Explore the qualities, texture, feel. Talk about creatures such as gnomes, imps, fairies, leprechauns. How do they move and sound?

Finish dance/motion sessions with quiet, slow motions ending at rest. Fold and collect nettings (scarves, etc.) or direct children to store in containers.

Scarf Dancing

up ↑ 3

- Use scarves and netting to show various emotions/moods. Discuss colors. What does yellow make you think of? Feel like? How would you dance purple? Black? White? What kind of music would you want?

- Read a story or poem. Use scarves to improvise costumes to dramatize the plot.

- Inflate a balloon. Let the air out slowly. Ask children to make the same motions using the scarves. Let the balloon fly and deflate suddenly. Copy the motions.

- Crumple, toss, float and snap scarves. Combine with drums played by other children. Scarves react to the drum sounds through motions.

Scarf Flowers

up ↑ 4

Each child has two scarves, one green and one of another color, representing stems and leaves and blooms of flowers.

- Children make the motions of sprouting, leafing, budding and blossoming flowers. Fully grown blossoms then make motions such as wilting, blowing in the wind, bending, swaying, etc.

- Flowers combine in various colors and shapes suggested by teacher and the children.

- Create foliage and blossoms using only hand motions by pulling out the scarves, held tightly in fists, so they gradually appear from in between the fingers.

- Combine scarf flowers with the dragon activity in dramatic play motions.

Caterpillar—Cocoon—Butterfly (Puppet/Finger Play)

5 ↑ 3

- Use cloth work gloves. Attach furry fabric to right glove (caterpillar). Attach wings and glue some glitter or sequins to the left glove (butterfly).

- Use motions to act out the finger play:

  a. Both hands behind back. Right hand slowly creeps out:

  "I'm so-o-o tired." Open thumb and forefinger in a yawn.

  "I'm going to sleep." Caterpillar crawls up and down, curls into a cocoon and goes behind the back saying, "I'll wake up and be a butterfly."

  b. After a pause—butterfly flutters out.

- Finger play of caterpillars and butterflies.

  "Let's go to sleep."

  The little caterpillar said.

  They tucked themselves into their beds.

  (fold fingers into palm)

  They will awaken bye and bye.

  (slowly unfold and hold up fingers)

  Each one will be a lovely butterfly.

LANGUAGE—DRAMA

Consonants (Reading Readiness)

- Say the name of an object, beginning with a specific consonant, i.e. "T"—towel, tray, teacher. Show the letter "T".

- Practice saying the "T" sound. Demonstrate the difference between "T", "P", "V".

- Ask the children to find or name objects beginning with a certain consonant.

Pick-A-Flower (Letters/Numerals, Reading Readiness)

- Draw flowers, write letters (or a numeral) on one side. Attach to popsicle stick "stems." Cut slits to fit stems in a shoe box cover. "Plant" the flowers in the "garden."

- Child picks a flower, tells the name of the letter.

- Number the flowers (1-10). Child picks one at a time and arranges in order. Use with letters and arrange alphabetically.

Pen and Picture Pals

Compose a class letter and mail to children of the same age group in another center or to a senior center/nursing home. Exchange recipes, poems, pictures, etc. Develop a regular correspondence and, if the center is near, plan for an exchange visit when the writers have become well acquainted by mail.

Picnic Talk (Verbal Skills)

Spread a blanket on the floor for an imaginary picnic. Ask each one: "What will you bring?" (Encourage complete sentences in response.) Make a list of items suggested. Find or draw pictures of picnic items. Can children remember which items they suggested?

Restaurant Game

- Make menus using food pictures, 3 to 6 each. Paste on paper plates.
- Make cards with single food items, i.e. bread, milk, fish, fruit, spaghetti.
- Child draws food cards to find matches on the menu.
- "Waiter" asks: "May I take your order?" Goes to "kitchen" to ask "cook" for "1 sandwich, 1 milk, 1 apple."
- "Cook" finds the items. "Waiter" serves to "diner."

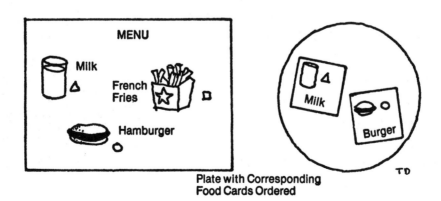

Plate with Corresponding
Food Cards Ordered

Food—From Farm to Table

Show pictures of foods growing, in production and processing, on sale, being cooked, being served. Example: a cow, grassy field, milking machine, barn, bottling, milk man or market, glass of milk on a table.

Mix up the pictures and ask children to put them in order.

CREATIVE PROJECTS

Stand-up Animals

Paste or draw animal pictures on folded paper. Add fuzzy cloth, cotton balls, yarn tails, etc.

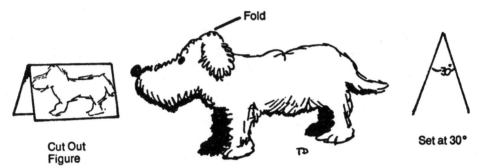

Fold

Cut Out
Figure

Set at 30°

Cork Animals

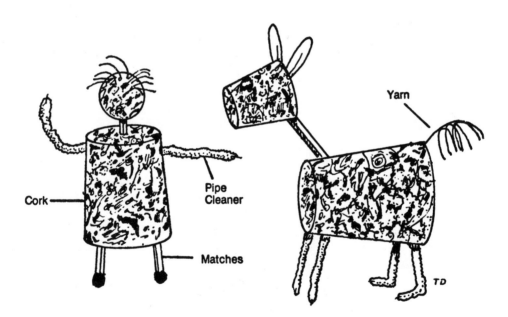

Cork

Pipe
Cleaner

Matches

Yarn

Mini-Dragons (Multi-cultural)

* Use blocks of styrofoam, spools, tubes. Lace together with twine, use sections of straw or beads in between sections. Add pipe cleaner legs, antennae; add scales and features. Attach pull string.

* Cover small boxes and cartons with scales using egg carton cups. Paint green and add features. Attach pull string. TODDLERS pull dragons in parades.

Caterpillar/Dragon

up ↑ 5

Cut six leg holes (1/2") in the lid of an egg carton.

Roll up newspaper, about 7" long and thick enough to fit the leg holes. Bend and put legs through holes, side by side until all leg holes are filled. Bend leg ends for feet. Add head, antennae and a pull string.

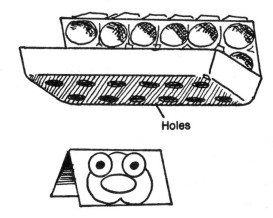

Holes

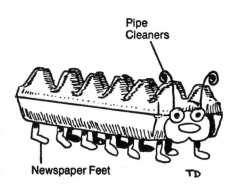

Pipe Cleaners

Newspaper Feet

Asian Costume

up ↑ 4

- Sun hat. Cut cardboard circles, 15" to 20" in diameter. Trace around circle shapes on wallpaper, oak tag and other colorful stiff papers. Decorate with flowers, designs and ribbons.

- Cut a slit to the center and overlap slit edges to form a cone hat. Attach ribbon ties.

- Kimono. Cut caftan shapes from folded cloth panels—sheets, curtains, pillow cases. Tie with sashes.

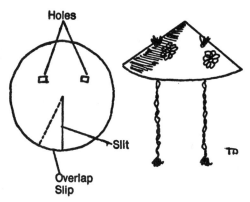

Holes

Slit

Overlap Slip

Boy-Girl Day (Multi-cultural)

up ↑ 3

Asians celebrate and fly fish kites, called koinbori (paper fish). Fly one kite for each child and celebrate with a parade of kites flown from sticks.

Cut two sheets of crêpe, tissue or painted newspaper into a fish shape. Tape or staple around edges, leaving an opening to stuff fish with crushed paper scraps. Seal opening and attach to a stick.

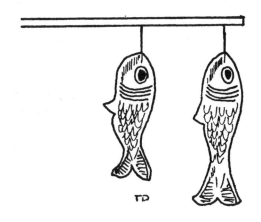

<u>JUST FOR FUN</u>

 ### *May Box Picnic*
- Decorate small boxes and baskets. Make a lunch for two to go in each one.
- Children from one group put their names (or draw pictures) into a May basket. Each child in the second group draws a name or picture and shares the picnic lunch with that child.
- Lunches might also be shared with a visiting parent.

 ### *May Poles (Multi-cultural)*
- Punch holes in a circle of cardboard and nail to the end of a dowel so it can turn. Tie ribbons, cloth strips or crêpe streamers in the holes.
- Children take turns holding the pole while others walk around it, winding and unwinding the streamers around the pole.
- Make mini-May poles. Tie or tack ribbons and paper streamers to dowels or pencils. Add tiny bells. Use as rhythm sticks, shakers and twirlers.

Toss Cups (Multi-cultural)
Attach a button or 1" wooden bead to the end of a paper cup with a string. Toss and catch the button in the cup.

May Baskets (Multi-cultural)
Some European countries celebrate May Day with May Pole Dances and May baskets.

Decorate small boxes, tubs, folders and cups. Pick or make flowers to fill the May baskets. Use May baskets as gifts for mothers and other special people.

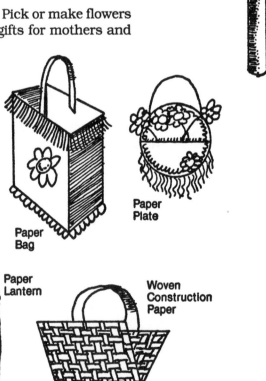

Streamers

Small Flower

Small Bead

12" Dowell

Margarine Tub

Onion Bag

Paper Bag

Paper Plate

Cardboard Folder

Paper Lantern

Woven Construction Paper

SEQUENCE TEN

JUNE

JUNE THEMES

JUNE

Circus Clowns, Pom Poms and Blot Bugs

It's June, when spring changes to **summer!** Let's **change the environment**—inside and outside. Children can help to **sort, mend and store** some things until autumn, switch things around and put old things to new uses. Can the housekeeping area be the **circus** and the blocks be built into **animal cages** for a zoo?

Our world is filled with **entertainment**. Do children realize that entertaining and sports are occupations? **Singing** and **dancing, acting, clowning, playing sports,** telling stories and making cartoons for television are all real "work" that seems to be play. There are hundreds of other jobs done behind the scenes to help **people who entertain**—camera and boom operators, costumers, script writers, make-up and hair specialists.

Entertainers, newscasters, comedians, etc. have real families, homes, children, gardens and pets—just like people who work in offices and factories or take care of young children.

Some entertainers are also **fathers**. All fathers are "entertainers" at home—bouncing babies on laps; giving pony rides on their backs; reading stories and dabbing shaving cream on little noses. Let's give a cheer and big applause for **Dads!**

Children will paddle and splash in wading pools, dig in beach sand, take boat rides and swimming lessons. Almost everyone will find some way to play in **water**. But whether **floating cork boats** in a dish pan while sitting on the cool grass or playing at the beach, tender skin, at all ages, needs protection with hats and **sunscreen**.

Baby birds have learned to fly and splash in a **bird bath**. Parent birds twitter and call to them. Can we imitate their **sounds**? **Bees** and **butterflies** flutter from flower to flower gathering **pollen**. Can we copy their **motions**, flying "over the rainbow" or through its **arch**?

Children can mix **lemonade** and make **rainbow sandwiches** for picnics; make **ice cream** and sample **berries** at a strawberry festival.

How long is the **number line** from corner to corner? How many different shapes will it take to make a shape walk from the sandbox to the wading pool? How many circus cars will we pull in a **circus train**? How big is an **elephant mural** filled with sawdust and **peanut shells**?

A huge **carton** with a curtain or TV "screen" becomes an **instant studio** for **talent** and **puppet shows** and **newscasts**. **Hoops, rings** and carton cages take their place under the Bigtop Circus. The ringmaster leads a **parade** of performers with a band of **"hummer-drummers"** and **clowns**. **Pom-poms** for everyone!

Children display special gifts (for Dad?), **book marks, string holders** and **decorated rock paperweights**. ("I made two, one for Dad and one for me!")

Outside, a carton village serves many events—Serendipity Day, Peanut Day and Clown Day.

Did ants come to taste the rainbow sandwiches at your picnic? Next time—JUST FOR FUN—scare them away with **Giant Insects** and **Blot Bugs**! Then **plan a party** and celebrate with a delicious **carousel cake**.

SEQUENCE TEN

PEOPLE

Fathers

5
↑
3

- Fathers perform many kinds of jobs, at home and work. Ask children to name and describe the work their fathers perform.

- Make "My Father's Jobs" books with pictures from magazines and newspapers. As children look at pictures they say, "My father can do that!" Write down the activity and/or cut and paste the picture.

- Compose a mural showing fathers' jobs. When a father comes to the center his child points to the pictures showing his work. Children applaud the father.

- Ask fathers to supply pictures relating to their jobs and add them to the mural.

Musicians

up
↑
3

Ask: What do musicians do? Where? Name some different kinds (trumpeters, drummers, pianists, etc.).

- Show a video tape of an orchestra or a band. Name the different instruments as they are played. After the children have seen this enough times to match sounds with instruments, you can ask them to identify the instruments on an audio tape.

- Children mime playing instruments as you name them—piano, trumpet, violin, drums, harp, etc.

- Play popular, folk, and symphonic music. Can the children identify each one? Move to the rhythms of different kinds of music. Mime happy, sad, silly, dramatic music.

Clowns

up
↑
3

Ask: "What do clowns do?—Why?" (Make us laugh.) "Name some funny people. Do you know people who make you laugh? Are they clowns?"

Encourage laughter and clowning/fun-making. Ask children to do something funny.

Talk about the difference between clowning and teasing. Dramatize poems and stories about clowning and joking.

Clowns

> *At a circus*
>
> *I saw the clowns*
>
> *Some were happy*
>
> *Some wore frowns*
>
> *Some had floppy hats*
>
> *Some wore crowns*
>
> *One wore rags*
>
> *Some wore ladies' gowns*
>
> *The sad,*
>
>> *The happy*
>>
>>> *The silly clowns!*

By Cléa Chmela

up
↑
4

Newscasters

- Listen to a news cast and discuss what makes news, i.e. events, people, happenings.
- Ask children to name the places, sports, towns, animals, etc. they see. Were there stories about children? Were the places familiar?

EXPANDING OUR WORLD

up
↑
3

Musical Performances

- Invite musicians to visit and play and/or sing.
- Watch for opportunities to hear live music where young people, especially, are playing instruments (bands, parades) or singing (chorus, musical shows).

up
↑
4

Newsroom

Visit a local TV newsroom. Notice different departments—news, weather, sports, etc.

What kinds of things do the children see that aren't found in most jobs? Microphones, lights, cameras, weather map, etc. (See LANGUAGE—DRAMA—*News At School*)

SKILLS FOR DAILY LIVING

up
↑
4

Sorting and Storing

Children help to organize and share the tasks of putting away toys and games which will be stored during the summer. This can be a one to two week process.

- Sort into categories—puzzles, lotto games, small cars.
- Empty and wash storage containers.
- Store seasonal items not used in summer.
- Unpack and shelve new supplies.

Seasonal Transitions and Changes—It Happened!

On the first day of summer vacation, the children who were returning to the center for the summer arrived to find the walls bare, the furniture pushed into one corner and piled up. The cleaners and painters had redone the room.

The staff might have resettled the rooms, hung pictures and set up activity centers before the children arrived. Instead, they deliberately left things bare and called the children to a meeting to help plan their own environment and summer program.

The teacher said, "This is your center. How would you like to have it? Should we put things back as they were? What changes could you suggest?"

Ideas began to pop! Following discussion and a plan chosen by the group, all became involved in rearranging and moving furniture.

David said, "Gee, this is really heavy. I don't think this can go through the door." "Maybe if we tip it it won't be so square," suggested Mary. "It's going to seem funny not to see the doll corner in the same place," another mover said.

As the days passed, other changes were made and with each move the staff observed learning:

"This is too heavy to go up the stairs." "There used to be room enough for four people, now only two at a time should be in here."...

up ↑ 2　Sun Protection

People and plants need sunlight, but *too much* sun can be dangerous to people, causing sunburn and heat prostration.

- Ask parents to send sunscreen lotion or cream with child's name on it. Use if children are going on a field trip that will mean being in the sun longer than usual (beach, zoo, etc.).

  Note: To be effective, sunscreen must be applied 30 minutes before exposure to sun.

- Make paper sun hats (or children may bring in sun hats) to wear whenever they will be outside. (See May—CREATIVE PROJECTS—*Asian Costume*)

- Provide liquids often—water, fruit juice—to prevent dehydration.

CONCEPTS

up ↑ 4　Past and Future

- LOOK BACK—Ask children: "What did you like best during the past week? (Month, spring, year)

  Make collage posters based on themes of past activities and events. Example: Best Day, Field Trip, Holiday Party.

- LOOK AHEAD—Ask: "What will you do in summer? Where will you go to school in September? What will we do next week?"

up ↑ 4　Number Line (Before/After) (Math)

Make a number line with masking tape on the floor and space numbers along the line. Ask children to: Stand on 5; stand on the one BEFORE 5; AFTER 6; move to a smaller number. Walk on every other number. Walk on the numbers missed and say them out loud.

up ↑ 3　Rainbow/Prism

- Read *A Rainbow of My Own* by Don Freeman (pub. Viking), and introduce a prism. Experiment with "catching" a rainbow reflection by placing a glass of water where the sun can shine through it and create a rainbow of colors.

- Hang a crystal where sun will strike it.

- Spray a hose into sunshine to cause rainbow effects.

- Divide a round table into wedge shapes. Mark each with swatches of rainbow colors.

  Ask children to find and sort objects onto the color patches.

- Ask children to tell you what colors they see in a picture of a rainbow.

up ↑ 4　Arches

- Point out the *shape* of a rainbow and tell children it is an arch. Ask if they can think of any other places where they have seen arches.

- On a neighborhood walk, look for arches in doorways, window frames, garden trellises, etc.

- SCHOOL AGE children can draw rainbows using a pencil compass, making the arc (or arch) smaller each time they draw a half-circle.

<u>SCIENCE</u>

Ice Cream

Many young children have never experienced making ice cream using a hand cranked mixer. The process takes about an hour. Divide into teams, taking turns at the crank.

Make ice cream from recipes in cookbooks or use commercial mixes.

TODDLERS can make ice cream, too. Put 2 cups heavy cream 3/4 cup sugar, 1 egg and 1/2 tsp. vanilla into a 1 lb. coffee can and seal top. Nest in 3 lb. coffee can in which crushed ice and 1 lb. table salt has been layered. Seal. Children roll back and forth on the floor for about 1/2 hour. Open and check every 5–10 minutes, and scrape down sides.

Berry Festival

Serve several kinds of seasonal berries—strawberries, blueberries, raspberries.

- Close your eyes and identify by taste, smell, and touch.
- Cook, drain off juice and use as paint.
- Use berry juices to flavor lemonade (below).
- Show real branches, plants, vines and stalks of the berry plants.
- Pick berries.

Rainbow Sandwiches

a. Mix cream cheese with food coloring to create four or more colored spreads. Mash in fresh fruits for flavor.

b. Using thin-sliced bread, spread a different color on each slice.

c. Stack slices of bread, fill layers with spread, and cut into sandwiches about two inches wide, so all the colors will show.

Lemonade

- Make lemonade from scratch using whole lemons. Compare with frozen and bottled.
- Make lemonade, divide into three or four portions and add food colors to each . Do they each taste the same?
- Use berry juices to color. Compare taste with food colored mixture.

Frog/Toad (Or Other Small Animal) Hunt

- Divide into groups, choose different areas, find and count frogs or toads, or other small animals common in the area.
- After a rainfall look for earthworms. Why did they come to the surface?
- Dig in a two foot square area of loamy soil to about one foot deep. Count earthworms.
- Dig in a sandy or clay soil. Count the earthworms. Compare the difference.

Bird Bath

Fasten a shallow container about 18" in diameter (trash can lid) to a fairly high pole. Keep about 1" of water in it for the birds to drink and bathe.

Try to place where children can see birds from a window.

⬆ up 5 **_Black Top Vs. Grass (Ecology, Conservation)_**

On a hot day, do the same activity (painting, a story, or game, etc.) on a paved area and on grass.

Discuss the difference. Explore both areas—lie down, sit and walk in bare feet (test first). Pour water on the ground. Measure the temperature at the surface.

Ask: Why do we need trees, grass, parks and woods?

⬆ up 5 **_Pollen and Nectar_**

Ask: What is pollen? Do insects (bees) eat it? What is nectar?

- Shake flower blossoms over a sheet of paper to collect pollen.

- Pull flowers/petal segments from the bud. The nectar sac is at the "socket" end. Taste nectar from a clover or day lily segment. Nectar is collected, carried to the nest (hive) and used to feed baby insects. Bees make honey from the nectar.

- When bees alight on flowers, the tiny hairs on their legs and body pick up pollen. As the bees fly from flower to flower, the pollen mixes with other pollen and fertilizes the plants.

- Put flour in center of paper flowers for pollen. Stand flowers in container (vases). Use egg-cup bees (See CREATIVE PROJECTS—*Bumble Bees*) with pipe cleaner legs to show how bees pick up pollen.

MUSIC—MOVEMENT

5 ⬆ 3 **_Baby Bird_**

Pretend: "A baby bird has fallen from its nest. Creep softly, quietly up to the bird. Gently pick it up and carry, climb and lift the baby back into its nest."

Let another child be the mother bird, alarmed, frightened and scolding. After baby is back in the nest the "mother" cares for it.

5 ⬆ 3 **_Toe Tickling_**

- Children pretend they are barefoot, walking on grass, hay, pavement, stepping on pebbles, mossy stones, prickers, icy stream water, hot sand, in mud, etc.

- Wiggle, creep, crawl and flutter. Make insect sounds—buzz, whirr, click—use the Hummer-Drummer (below). (See CREATIVE PROJECTS in this sequence for suggestions to make insects.)

4 ⬆ 2 **_Hummer-Drummer_**

Cut a hole 3" long and 1" wide in a paper towel tube, 3" to 4" from one end. Wrap waxed paper around the tube over the hole. Tape securely.

Cut a round of waxed paper and wrap over one end. Secure with tape.

Hum into the open end of the tube. Tap the sides lightly to create vibrations and amplify humming sounds.

Note: Do not let children share mouth toys or instruments. Make and identify one for each child.

Bee Work (Colors)

- Make large flowers from cardboard. Paint petals in various colors (rainbow shades). Paint the centers yellow. Make a set of smaller flowers, or colored cards, to match the large flowers.

- Lay the large flowers on the floor. Children (bees) choose a small flower and find the match, making buzzing bee sounds and motions as they fly to pollinate the blooms.

Zoo Walk

- Show pictures of zoo and circus animals. Child chooses an animal, names it and makes the motion and sound of the animal.

- Play "I am Going to the Zoo." Ask: "How will you go?"

  1st child: "I will hop."

  2nd child: "I will hop and jump."

  3rd child: "I will hop, jump and spin."

  4th child: "I will hop, jump, spin and run." Etc.

Circus (Hoops and Rings)

- Divide into small groups. Each group chooses a trainer who chooses an animal to be portrayed. Teachers guide trainers in planning acts for their animals.

- Use hoops or mark rings on the floor and each group takes a turn entertaining others with animal acts. Teachers (ringmasters) use a whistle to start and stop acts. Animals scurry to cages (blanket tents, cartons, or under tables).

- Some children play instruments and make sound effects.

- Set up a display of stuffed animals in carton cages.

- Clowns tumble, somersault and do silly tricks between animal acts. (See also JUST FOR FUN—*Clown Day*)

LANGUAGE—DRAMA

Talent Show

Develop a talent show—a week long project to plan and carry out. (See also JUST FOR FUN—*Planning a Party*)

- Discuss theater manners such as arriving on time; being polite, listening and not talking during performances; applauding; not shifting seats; etc.

- Choose and gather props; arrange seats and stage area; hang a curtain; set up and equip a booth with tickets and play money.

- Make popcorn and juice drinks for a refreshment counter.

- Make signs and invitations for parents and other guests.

- Decide on program and various acts and performers. Teachers encourage children to demonstrate simple skills and talents, choosing one or two to perform, such as:

  "Amy makes beautiful clay bunnies. She can show us how."

  "Julio can sing a song in Spanish about a fish."

  "Jordana can walk along the ladder rungs and balance."

  "Chiu Lin writes his name in Chinese characters."

- Children are involved in managing and running the show.

June

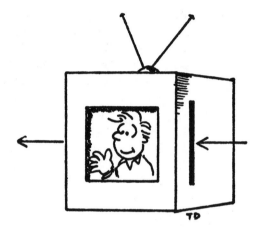

News At School

`up ↑ 5`

Reporters, equipped with home-made mikes, go around room (local) and center (regional) to collect news. They return and report events. "Josh built a road which completely filled the block corner." "Susan fell and had first aid treatment on a scraped knee." "Joan's picture of sea life is hanging in the lobby." "The new baby at Jeremy's house is visiting with his mother in the nursery."

- Divide into teams to prepare reports, draw illustrations, maps and portraits of animals and people. Include reports on weather, music, activities and projects, lunches, visitors, accidents, etc.

- Tour with a camera. When film is developed, show the pictures and ask the children, "What was happening?" (See CONCEPTS—*Past and Future*)

VIPs and Entertainers

`up ↑ 5`

This activity and the previous one could be combined with *Newscasters*—EXPANDING OUR WORLD.

- Make a TV from a carton. Cut a square for the screen, cut two slits in opposite sides just behind the screen, stick knitting needles into a ball of clay for the antenna.

- Mount pictures of famous people (president, children's entertainers and cartoon characters). "Project" the pictures on the television screen by pushing through slots. (See illustration) Children take turns projecting and guessing.

- Show circus animals, letters, shapes, etc.

- Project a sequence of pictures which tell a story. Ask a child to narrate as pictures are shown.

- Show an entertainer (ballerina, clown, juggler). Ask children to describe the actions each might use.

Fish School (Reading Readiness)

`5 ↑ 4`

- Discuss a "school" of fish. Make a giant fish and paste or draw upper case letters on it.

- Make small fish for individual letters, several fish for each letter. Attach paper clips to the small fish. Cut letters from ads, cereal cartons, magazines, etc. Use in sorting and spelling activities.

- Fish for small fish with magnets on lines. Match to the letters on the big fish.

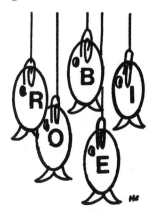

Talents and Skills (Game)
up ↑ 3 Make cards showing skills and talents—sweeping, zipping, pouring, cutting, skipping, walking on a narrow plank, etc.

- Child draws a card, demonstrates the skill. The *child* decides if "success" was achieved. Child keeps and counts successes, or, returns card to pile to "try again later."

- Encourage children to choose some skills they do best and to try others which need practice. When a child succeeds in a new skill say, "You could not do that last time, now you can!"

CREATIVE PROJECTS

up ↑ 4 ***Fathers' Gifts***

- Make spoon book marks. Draw faces with markers, wrap on felt or cloth coats, and glue on yarn hair.

- Make paperweights or door stop creatures. Choose rocks which resemble figures, faces, creatures. Decorate with oil or acrylic paints. Varnish or polymer spray will help preserve the paint. Encourage children to paint one for a gift and another for themselves.

- Make string holders. Use coffee cans, oatmeal cartons, small sturdy boxes, etc. Decorate with felt, paint, yarns, and trims to create faces. Decorate lids as hats. Make holes in tops (cans) or sides (cartons) to dispense string.

up ↑ 4 ***Giant Insects***

Create insects from large folded cardboard/oaktag. Decorate with paint, elegant junk (wire, pipe cleaners, cotton balls, beads, buttons, sequins, yarn).

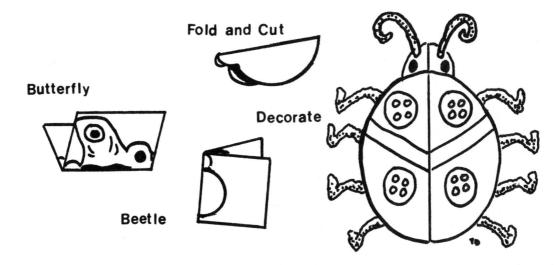

Fold and Cut

Butterfly

Decorate

Beetle

up ↑ 4 ***Blot Bugs***

Drop blobs of paint in the center of paper. Fold and rub. Unfold and dry. Add insect features to the shape—wings, legs, antennae. Cut and hang on strings.

June

Bumble Bees

- Glue, tape or staple (manual skills) two egg cup sections together. Paint yellow. Dry. Add black strips, face, wings and pipe-cleaner feet.
- Tie to a stick. *Or:* suspend several as a mobile *or* hang on a branch.

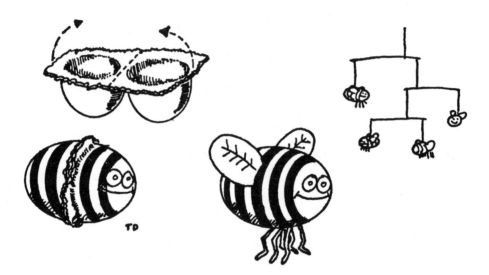

Circus Projects

Peanut Elephant

Draw a large elephant shape on mural paper. Fill the shape with glued on peanut shells. Shelling peanuts, separating nuts from shells, cracking the shells and gluing them is excellent small muscle activity.

Peanut Finger Puppets

Break peanut shells in half to form thimbles, making one for each finger. Put a face on each shell with ink. Place a shell face on each finger tip and make conversation with puppets.

Circus Train

- Cut or draw pictures of circus animals on rectangles of paper (train cars). Paste strips of black paper over the picture to make cages. Add circles (wheels). Decorate edges with scrolls and fancy borders.
- Hang the cars along wall in a train.
- Variation: Make cars on folded paper with pictures on both sides. Hitch cars together with string and pull the train.

Pom Poms

- Wind yarn around cardboard 3"x5". Tie the loops on one end. Cut the loops on the opposite end. Remove the cardboard.
- Ravel sweaters, mittens, etc. and use yarn to make "crinkly" pom poms.

(See also March—MUSIC—MOVEMENT—*Bunny Wiggle*)

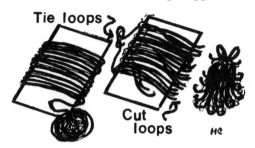

Clowns (Shapes, Following Patterns)

- Put out assorted paper shapes—circles, triangles, rectangles. Ask children to make a clown following the pattern of the illustration.
- Vary by using cloth shapes.
- Another time ask: "What else can you make using the shapes?"

Sawdust Animals and Sculpture (Recipe)

Create animals from sawdust. Paint with tempera. Put in small box "cages," painted and decorated as circus cars.

Sawdust Recipes

A. 2 cups sawdust

1 cup wheat paste

water to make a *thick* mixture

B. 1 part flour or wheat paste

2 parts water

Heat until clear and thick. Cool.

Add fine sawdust to make a thick modeling material.

C. Mix sawdust with liquid glue to a thick paste.

Mixture can be modeled or spread flat on waxed paper and cut into shapes.

Material can be sawed, filed, whittled or sanded.

Boats from Corks and Plastic Tubs (Magnets)

- Float corks to determine how they will set in the water.

Pound small steel nails or tacks into one end. Tie small magnets to string or attach to short sticks to attract and pull boats.

- Use margarine tubs and slice plastic bottles lengthwise to make boats. Attach paper clips along edges and pull with magnets as above.

June

JUST FOR FUN

Bubbles from a Can

up ↑ 3

Cut out both ends of cans. Smooth edges.

Children dip cans in bubble solution and sweep through the air to create bubbles.

(See September—JUST FOR FUN—*Bubbles* and August—JUST FOR FUN—*Window Pane Bubbles*)

Carton Village (On-going)

up ↑ 4

Stimulate dramatic play and games outside. Make various buildings from large cartons and blanket tents. Make signs —Fire Station, Grocery Store, Police Station, School, Hospital, Garage. Line off roads and make traffic signs.

Clown Day/Mini Circus

up ↑ 2

(See also MUSIC—MOVEMENT—*Circus*)

Rope

Coffee or Paint Can

* Paint clown faces on children.

* Dress in costumes and march in a parade. Pull the circus train.

* Make an obstacle course for acrobats—planks to walk, ladders, ropes and chalk lines to walk on. Decorate a long pole with streamers to use as a balance pole.

* Children are animals and trainers. Animals have tails, ears, trunks, gloves with paper claws, etc. Trainers wear capes.

* Children use puppets, stuffed animals, school pets or pictures as props to tell about an animal, i.e. "This is Hazel. She is a hamster. We feed her carrots."

Stilts

up ↑ 5

Tie loops of rope through large cans. Rope loops should be long enough to be held taut when children stand on the cans.

Serendipity Day

up ↑ 3

Set up a series of numbered activities, inside and outside. Each activity has a set of tickets with matching numbers. Children draw tickets and go to the activity.

Suggestions: Popping corn; making blot pictures; having a stilt trail race; crawling through an obstacle course; making figures from marshmallows and toothpicks; playing a game; listening to a story in a blanket tent; blowing bubbles; painting rocks; finding items on a treasure hunt; mixing punch; etc.

Each child does only two or three activities, drawing a new ticket before each one. Child draws again if a duplicate ticket is drawn.

Peanut Day

up ↑ 3

Begin with a peanut hunt—inside and outside. An easy way to do this is to scatter nuts in the grass. After peanuts have been gathered, use them in a variety of peanut and shell activities. See suggestions in this sequence.

Variations: White Rock Day; Pine Cone Day; Box Day; Circle Day; Paper Doll Day; Game Day; Paper Bag Day.

Party Planning (Skills for Daily Living)

Plan a series of activities to be carried out in a sequence to give a party. Begin in the morning to plan an afternoon party, or, begin on Monday for a Friday party.

Some suggestions:

- Decide on a theme, colors, foods, games, music.
- Make invitations, decorations, favors, refreshments.
- Plan and practice entertainment.
- Make a check list and mark off completed tasks.
- Assemble materials and distribute to areas where they will be used.
- Rearrange space as needed to accommodate party activities.
- Clean and dust to "get ready for company."
- Make a guest book for all to sign.

Carousel Cake

Bake a round cake, frost, and stand animal crackers around the edge. Turn on a lazy Susan as it is served.

Play a music box.

Older children, using a cake mix, may do all of the above.

CREATIVE movement is used to follow up, expand and reinforce concepts throughout the daily program.

SEQUENCE ELEVEN

JULY

JULY THEMES

JULY

Sun Dials and Spider Tales

During July (and August) at many child care centers, the program may need to extend to include older children. The age span of staff members may also widen as volunteers and teenagers are added as counselors and assistants. All ages assist and guide each other, working and **living together as a family**. Two children work closely together to create **partner portraits** and both share mutual responsibility as **swimming buddies** to keep each other **safe in the water**.

Africa is far away. **Outer space** is way beyond! But, undaunted, we can blast off from our **space stations** to see the **stars** and **planets**; we can launch **balloon jets** and land our **space ship** on the **moon** and have a picnic! We can mix soup from **dehydrated mixes** and eat **dried fruits** just like real astronauts. "Space foods" were not invented by NASA scientists, they took their cues from tribal cultures and pioneers who used dried foods as they **blazed wilderness trails** and stored food for the long winters.

Hikes to a nearby park or just across the playground to a make believe jungle require hearty snacks. We can make **trail mix** and sample juicy **melons**. Children who will enter school in the fall can practice **sandwich making** skills for lunch boxes and back packs.

How did **pioneers** and **tribal people** "tell time?" Perhaps they used the sun. Children can use a string compass to make a **sun dial**, then watch its shadow to calibrate the time. **African tribes** used **instruments made from natural materials** to send messages. Children can use such instruments and **body language** to express emotions; they can think about **feelings** suggested by musical sounds and make designs to express feelings. They can also decide "Who's the **boss** of my body?"

Africans tell **Anasi folktales** in **Swahili**. Our "tribal groups" might send messages using a few Swahili words.

Water and **soil projects** might include experiments with **wetness** and **absorption**; **capillary action; aqua terrariums;** making **dip nets** and using **waterscopes**. What do terrarium creatures eat? What is **insect food?**

Inside and outside, artists create **sand paintings, alligator bottles, string designs, tie-dyed banners, plaster pins, clothespin** and **rock-nik people** (from moon rocks?). Just like pioneers and Africans, we can stitch patchwork and **weave grass**.

Children plan **Backwards Day, Puppet Day,** or a **Carnival Day** with games of chance— JUST FOR FUN!

SEQUENCE ELEVEN

PEOPLE

up ↑ 4

Partner Portraits

Children work in pairs to create portraits of one another. Note their observation of characteristics—hair color and style, skin and eye color, clothing colors and patterns.

Children trace around each other (lying down on large paper) and, with help as needed, cut out figures.

Paint features, add yarn or paper strip hair. (Wrap paper strips around pencils to curl.)

Attach cloth and paper clothing, accessories, buttons, jewelry and ribbons.

Hang portraits along a wall. Use for "Who Am I?" and other guessing games.

up ↑ 4

Guides/Rangers/Lifeguards

Guides: Lead people on camping trips in the wilderness.

Rangers: Take care of national and state parks and help campers and vacationers who are ill, lost, hurt.

Lifeguards: Work at beaches and swimming pools.

- Children talk about experiences they have had.
- Role play the jobs of the above people.
- Stress safety aspects such as staying on marked trails; picking up litter and protecting wildlife; putting out campfires; obeying posted rules.

up ↑ 4

Astronauts

What do they do? Where do they go? How do they travel?

Use props and costumes to develop ideas with dramatic play. Extend children's ideas with stories, films and sound effects.

Compare space activity, preparation, training and survival techniques with hiking and mountain climbing. Children may bring some equipment from home—back packs, helmets, thermos, flashlights, etc.—to use in play activities.

EXPANDING OUR WORLD

up ↑ 4 — *Settlers, Hunters, Frontier People (Multi-cultural)*

Talk about people who settled your area. How did they live? Eat? What did they wear? How did they travel?

- Make lean-to shelters with cardboard (bark), leafy branches and boughs. Take lunches of biscuits spread with applesauce, apples, hard boiled eggs, some milk. A frontier settler might carry such a simple meal in a tin pail (coffee cans with twine handles).

- Gather wood for a pretend campfire. Roll up in blankets, sit around the fire and tell stories about the day's hike—"over mountains," "across grassy plains," "through dry gulches," "across rushing rivers."

- Make "Daniel Boone" style fringed vests and caps with brown bags and cloth.

up ↑ 4 — *Trail Marking, Camping and Hiking*

Explore a nearby park, playground or center play area. Establish a "base camp" where supplies, food, blankets are stored.

- Divide into teams. Explore, mark and name areas and trails—"Shady Glen," "Black River" (paved walks),"Slippery Slope" (slide), "Blue Lagoon" (wading pool). Mark trails with cloth strips, flags on sticks, painted stones.

- Return to camp for food and tell campfire tales about exploration.

up ↑ 4 — *Inside Trails and Settlements*

Rearrange inside areas and set up interest centers with frontier, camping, related themes. Redirect uses of equipment—blocks might be gold nuggets to be mined; the water table becomes the "Inland Lake"; a plank is the bridge across "Beaver Gap"; tables turn into shelters; housekeeping area is a frontier town or mining camp.

- Hook a line of small cartons together in supply trains. Make cloth hoods to form covered wagons for settlers. Pull wagons into a circle for snacks and stories.

- Mark trails between areas with chalk and tape lines, small stickers, string lines, foot prints. Use cardboard circles and rug squares to lay out stepping stones.

up ↑ 4 — *Sandbox Trails and Settlements*

Use sandbox and surrounding areas to "explore" and establish new settlements. Children decide where mountains, rivers, caves, lakes, deserts, forests, etc. will be located. Boulder cliffs, pebble roads, twig forests are added, replacing regular sandbox toys. Each area is given a special name—"Freda's Lake," "David's Cave," etc.

- Create people and animals from twigs, berries and clothespins. (See CREATIVE PROJECTS)

- Explorers and settlers decide each day who will make new trails, re-build settlements, work on mining teams, make forests, etc.

- When rains destroy settlements, discuss floods and other weather disasters which cause damage to real homes and landscape.

- Variation: Use shallow cartons of sand for settlements for individual children.

July

SKILLS FOR DAILY LIVING

 Lunch Making

Teach children to choose, prepare and pack nutritious lunches. Set some limits on the amounts and variety of foods chosen, but in general allow the children to decide on their own.

- Make practice "sandwiches." Tape together several layers of cardboard cut to bread slice size. Practice slipping into sandwich bags or wrapping with waxed paper.

- Practice spooning puddings and stewed fruits into containers and sealing with lids.

- Teach how to pack a lunch. Put heavy, dense foods (fruits, plastic containers, drink cans) on the bottom. Put soft, crunchy foods (crackers, chips) on the top.

- Offer two or three choices of sandwich fillings—some to spread and some to layer. Use plastic knives for spreads (margarine, salad dressing, peanut butter, cheese spreads).

    Offer vegetables and fruits—in pieces, or whole; chips, crackers, breads; cookies.

Water Safety

- Buddies. Always swim with a partner. Know where your partner is and call for help if your buddy is in trouble.

- Stay in safety zones. If swimming area is enclosed by ropes, stay inside those ropes! They are there to protect you.

- Don't tip the boat. Make a canoe out of heavy foil. Show what happens if you put a stone on one side.

- Always wear a life jacket in a boat. Fill two small cloth bags with pebbles. Fasten several corks to one of the bags. Drop them both into the water. What happens?

CONCEPTS

 Sundial (Before/After, Early/Late, Light/Dark)

Secure a 5'-6' dowel in a board or concrete base in an area of full sun during most of the day. Attach a 4'-6' long string by a loop to the base of the pole and tie a marking stick at the other end. Mark a circle around the pole. Outline the circle with pebbles, tape or paint, depending on the surface around the pole. Remove the string compass.

- Use an alarm clock, set at each hour, to calibrate the spots on the circle where the sun casts the shadow of the pole. Mark each hour spot with a large stone, brick or stake. (In one center, the children dug small holes at the hour spots, filled them with concrete and set small pebbles in the shape of numerals.)

- "A sundial works throughout the year because the sun, whether high or low, is always in the same direction at the same time of day." (*Sun and Light, An Action Science Book* by Neil Ardley (pub. Franklin Watts, Inc.)

Sand Painting (Colors, Long-term Project, African and Native American)

- Color sand in many shades using vegetable dyes and paints. Dry in the sun. Put in small plastic containers. Punch holes in tops to make shakers.

- Paint with thinned white glue a section of a design or picture, one color at a time, shake on colored sand. Dry. Paint glue on another area, add colored sand, dry. Continue process with each area.

    Work in shallow cartons. Show children how to funnel excess sand back into containers.

SCIENCE

Trail Mix

up ↑ 3

Provide bowls of food bits for children to choose and scoop into small containers of Trail Mix to take on hikes and tracking expeditions suggested in this sequence. Use coffee scoops and small measuring cups. Mark bowls with numerals to suggest how many servings of each item.

Cereal bits, nuts, raisins, chocolate and butterscotch bits, dried fruit bits, croutons, coconut.

Consult recipe books for various Trail Mix combinations.

Melons

up ↑ 4

Children use melon ball scoop to serve themselves two or three kinds of melon.

Taste-test melons. Guess which one when blindfolded.

Water Scope/Dip Net

up ↑ 4

- Water Scope—Submerge a large mouthed jar in water, open end down, to magnify and observe underwater life.

- Dip Net—Make by unbending a wire coat hanger. Shape it into loop about 6" in diameter. Twist the ends to form a handle about 14" long. With waxed string, stitch a sack of plastic or cloth netting around loop ring, or cut the end of a nylon stocking about 8-10" up from foot, fold top edge over loop and stitch or staple.

Amphibians (Pond, Stream and Swamp Animals)

up ↑ 4

Small amphibians can be kept in an aqua-terrarium.

(See also—May—SCIENCE—*Frogs*)

Where to find:

Newts, salamanders, turtles: still waters, swamps and ponds.

Efts, frogs, snakes: muddy banks and nearby woods and rushes.

Minnows, darters, mud puppies: clear pools and rocky crevices.

Crayfish: silty bottoms and under stones.

What to feed:

Newts, salamanders, baby turtles, mud puppies, tadpoles, crayfish: Raw meat, fish food, worms, chopped egg.

Frogs, toads, chameleons: Live flies, mealy bugs, meal worms.

Minnows and fresh water fingerlings: Earthworms, cooked meat, slugs, scraps, apples, cabbage, lettuce.

Snakes and lizards: Live salamanders, toads, insects dangled on a string. Don't keep small amphibians in the same cage with snakes and lizards.

Aqua-Terrarium

Use a rectangular aquarium or build a suitable tank. A good size is about 18" long, as wide as a standard 12" plank, and a foot high. You will need:

    a. Two pieces of glass, the same size, for side walls.

    b. One-inch redwood or cedar plank, 12" wide and 4' long.

    c. Twelve feet of 1/2" quarter round molding.

Cut piece of plank exactly as long as the glass. Cut two more pieces, each one foot long. These are the end pieces, nailed or screwed to the bottom plank, as shown. Cut eight pieces of molding in one-foot lengths and nail them inside edges of end pieces. Leave space between each pair of strips the thickness of the glass so the glass will slip easily into the slot. Slide glass into place. Place strip of molding along top of each side wall and nail the strip ends to the edges of the end boards.

Fill bottom of tank with layer of sand or gravel about one inch deep. (Ocean sand will kill the plants.) Then a layer of charcoal for good drainage, next a two or three inch layer of rich loamy soil dug from the woods. Shape the soil into hills and valleys with a high and dry area at one end of the tank. Rocks and stones can be added to build little ledges and caves to give shy creatures a dark, damp place to hide. At the low end, dig an excavation and install a pond. Put in a shallow glass or enamel baking dish about 6 or 8 inches square. Cover the bottom with pebbles and fill with water to a depth of about two inches. The pond should be a separate unit so it is easily removed for cleaning and freshening the water.

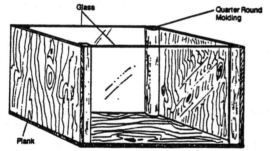
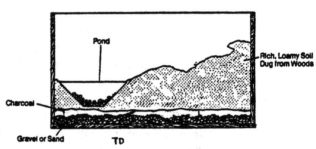

Insect Foods

Grasshopper, walking stick: Fresh grasses and weeds, clumps of sod in the cage, watered occasionally, will last several days. Put soil in the cage.

Beetles: Grubs, caterpillars, meal worms. A piece of rotten wood with soft insects in it. Provide a tin of water.

Crickets: Wet bread chunks, lettuce, peanut butter. Provide water and soil to dig in.

Caterpillars, tree hoppers: Leaves from the plant on which they are found. Lettuce leaves. When they start spinning a cocoon they no longer need food.

Praying Mantis: Gather small live insects by shaking a bush over newspaper; bits of raw chopped meat.

Grasshopper Greenhouse

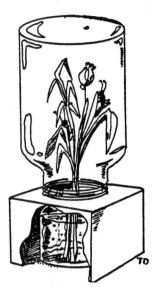

Fill a small jar with water and place a 4" deep cardboard box over it upside down. Punch a small hole in the center of the box and stick a few cut flower stems through it so the plants rise five or six inches above the box. Put the insects in a quart jar and turn it upside down over the plants so that the rim is resting on the box. This will give the hoppers a homey environment and will keep them from falling in the water and drowning. Replace with fresh greens periodically.

Soils

Teach the basic ideas such as:

The "weathering" of rocks by wind, sand, water, freezing, thawing, etc. forms sand and clay. Loam is made up of sand and clay. Some soil contains decaying vegetation (rotting plants) called humus.

- Which soils crumble in your hand? Which stick together? Which make mud?

- Sift soils from gardens, wooded areas, roadsides, sandboxes, beaches, plant pots. Sort and display.

- The earth's crust is made up of layers of rock covered with soil. Pile soils into small mounds. Pour water on them. What happens?

- Ask: How are different soils used? (Growing—loams; filtering and drainage—sand; building and paving, making concrete—sand and gravel; bricks—clay; pleasure—sand boxes and beaches.)

- Show soils which grow different kinds of plants (cactus and beach grass in sand compared to vegetables in loam and trees in humus). Pull up plants growing in different soils and look at root systems. (Teacher pulls or digs up *one* of each kind for the children to study.)

- Measure the sweetness or sourness (acidity) of soils, using litmus paper. "Press a strip of litmus paper into the soil. If the paper remains *blue* the soil is sweet, if it turns *red* there is too much acid in the soil. (Lime is used to "sweeten" acidic soil to enhance growth.)

- Compost is a fertilizer made from rotting and decaying matter and spread around plants to reduce evaporation, control weeds and improve the soil.

Rocks

Collect a variety of natural rocks and man-made or mined stones—slate, marble, granite, brick, concrete, coal. Study wet and dry. Look at them with a magnifying glass. Weigh. Sort by color.

- Drop vinegar on a limestone chip. What happens? Acid in vinegar reacts with the lime causing it to fizz and bubble. Experiment for lime content in other rocks.

- What rocks can be scratched with nails? (Hardness test)

- How are rocks used? Look for natural and man-made foundations, bridges, walkways, pavements, etc.

Irrigation, Erosion and Floods (Conservation)

- Supply materials for an irrigation project to bring water from a faucet to a garden, tree or grass. How many ways can we carry water?

  Use buckets, hoses, plastic sheets (to line ditches), etc.

- Pour water from different heights onto sand and loam to show erosion effects. Look for erosion damage on pavement edges and embankments. What prevents erosion?

- Make small earth dams. Add toy people and cars. Flood.

  Repeat using plastic or wooden dams. Show pictures of real dams and reservoirs; irrigation and sprinkling projects at farms.

- How can we save water? Stopping faucet drips, using water from wading pools to water plants.

Wetness /Absorption

Test the wetting powers of clear and soapy water.

- Soak a piece of yarn in clear water and another piece in soapy water. Remove and pull the strands apart. Which is wetter?

- Drop clear water from eye droppers onto swatches of different cloth—cotton (diapers), nylon, wool, netting. Observe differences.

  Repeat using soapy water.

- Drop clear and soapy water on other materials—wood, plastic, metal, glass. Are there differences?

- Let a cooking pot or dish with food residue (egg, cereal, tomato sauce) stand and dry. Try to clean with a damp sponge.

  Soak the dishes in clear and in soapy water. Compare the differences in cleaning.

- Soak two soiled garments (socks) in clear and in soapy water. Compare differences.

Dissolution

Hot liquids (water) dissolve dry ingredients faster than cold liquids.

- Stir a teaspoon of sugar into cold water until the sugar dissolves. Time experiment.

  Heat some water and repeat the experiment. Which sugar dissolves faster?

- Fold a paper cone so there is no opening at the bottom. Pour some sugar into the cone. Touch the tip of the cone. Taste. Is there any sweetness?

  Pour some water into the cone. Catch some of the water as it soaks through the sugar. Does it taste sweet?

Capillary Action

Stand the ends of celery stalks or light colored carnations in a glass containing colored water (about 2" deep). Observe in several hours and again the next day. What happens?

MUSIC—MOVEMENT

up ↑ 3 *Body Language*

Extend the ideas in LANGUAGE—DRAMA—*Bossing.*

- What part of your body can you use to pick up something? What part of your body can you use to wave? What part of your body can you use to push?

- Your hands are stuck together. Pull them apart. Your hands are stuck to your knees. Pull them away.

- Run without getting anywhere.

- Reach up on a shelf and get something. See if we can guess what, by asking questions about it.

up ↑ 3 *Instruments From Nature (Multi-cultural, Africa, Tribal Groups)*

Tribes from many cultures create rhythmic patterns and dances. Rhythm is often more important than melody in tribal music. Rhythms from Africa are the origin of American jazz. Create dances and chants about experiences, using instruments made from natural products.

Painted pebbles knocked together	Shaking leafy branches
Bark cups filled with gravel	Shaking bunches of grass
Hitting tree trunks	Shaking sticks of various sizes
Water in pools hit with sticks	Sticks striking stones
Shaking containers of water	Stones striking sticks

up ↑ 4 *Tambourine*

Make a hoop from sturdy cardboard or plastic. Cut slits and punch holes as shown in the illustration.

String, in pairs, metal washers, bottle caps, roofing disks, or other metal circles. Separate disks slightly by stringing a button between them. Allow enough slack in the stringing wire for the disks to rattle.

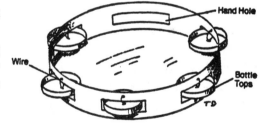

up ↑ 4 *Marimba (Africa, South America, Mexico)*

Nail, or tie, a row of small sticks, varying in diameter, across two supports. Lay on the ground or hang from a tree limb, over a carton or tub, or lean against a building. Rub with sticks to create sounds. Decorate the marimba and playing sticks with feathers, streamers and ribbons.

up ↑ 4 *Whistles From Reeds (or Straws)*

Pinch the end of a hollow reed (or straw) and make a diagonal cut to bring the end to a point. Blow through the reed to make sounds. Reeds cut in different lengths will make different sounds (pitches).

Maracas and Shakers (Africa, South America, Mexico)

- Use maracas and shakers in sensory games. Arrange by sounds. Guess the contents.
- Use in rhythmic pattern games.

Shakers:

- Punch bottle caps with nails and string on wire loops. Tape sharp edges of the wire.
- String buttons, plastic caps, washers to make ankle and wrist bracelets.
- Put metal washers on a bolt.
- Glue halves of nutshells together over twine. Tie 3 or 4 to a dowel handle.

Maracas:

- Put nut shells inside a plastic shaker.
- Seal plastic containers or dried gourds cut in half filled with: beans, sand, pebbles, rice, wood, plastic, glass beads, seeds,shells, styrofoam, or water.

LANGUAGE—DRAMA

African Names (Multi-cultural, Africa)

- Use African tribal names to develop trail and pioneer activities suggested above.
- Use in rhythmic and rhyming games.

African Tribal Names:

Ethiopian	Hausa	Kikuyu	Ndebele	Herero
Yoruba	Tuareg	Masai	Zulu	Watusi
Pygmy	Ashanti	Berber	Shilluk	Bushman

Swahili Words and Anasi Stories (Multi-cultural, Africa)

- Read *Moja Means One* and *Jamba Means Hello* by Muriel Feelings (pub. Dial Press). These books illustrate simple Swahili words.
- Read and tell *Anasi the Spider* stories, the basis of many African folk tales.
- Observe spiders. Develop Anasi stories based on the motions and habits of spiders .
- Make insect puppets for use in dramatic play and stories. (See CREATIVE PROJECTS—May and June)

Bossing

Adults instruct, train and direct young children—they might be called "bosses." Help the children to be their own bosses, to develop skills to know what, when, where and why they can control their actions and environment.

Ask: "What is inside your head that helps you think?" (Brain) "Your brain is like a control center. It sends messages to all parts of your body. *You* boss your own control center."

- Tell your body to jump, sit, bend, etc. Blink. Shout. Sing.
- Take turns "bossing." "Chi-chi, *tell* three people to carry the lunch trays." "Carl, *tell* two people to set the table."
- Discuss the difference between telling, asking, directing, guiding and bossing. Practice voice tones and gestures. Use dramatic play in pleasant and unpleasant ways of "bossing." (See also MUSIC—MOVEMENT—*Body Language*)

CREATIVE PROJECTS

Space Activities

 ### *Balloon Jets*

Stretch a fishing line or nylon string between two points, one low enough for the children to reach. String a 3" or 4" section of plastic drinking straw onto the line. Inflate a balloon and stick it to the straw section with a piece of masking tape folded sticky side out. Let go of the balloon so the escaping air will push straw and balloon along the line. This is one way to explain jet propulsion.

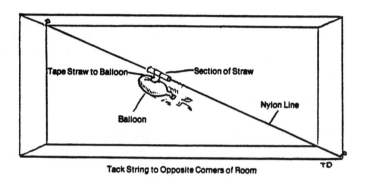

Tack String to Opposite Corners of Room

Space Food

Pioneers and early explorers developed dried foods which needed no refrigeration. Space explorers use such foods to limit weight on their journeys.

- Taste a variety of dried fruits.

- How many dried foods can children name? (Salad dressing and soup mixes, dried milk and potatoes, baking mixes, gelatins and puddings.)

  Ask: How are they all the same? (Liquid is added) Weigh before and after mixing with liquid. Compare weight of package of dried soup with canned soup.

- Purée vegetables and fruits. Put in plastic bags and demonstrate how astronauts squeeze foods from tubes.

 ### *Planetarium*

- Fasten black paper or cloth to the ceiling. Attach white or silver stars, some in the shape of constellations, i.e. Big and Little Dippers.

- Lie on the floor and use flashlights to pick out constellations.

- Construct satellites. Push dowels through styrofoam balls. Attach wires and pipe cleaners to coffee cans. (Such "satellites" are close to actual size of real communication satellites.)

July

Rocket Ship and Space Equipment

- Construct Rocket from appliance carton, attach nose cone, fins, insignias. Paint or cover with foil. Equip instrument panel and launch control center with knobs, dials, wires, spools, etc. Add timers and buzzers, bells and whistles.

- Make Space Helmets from paper grocery bags with viewing windows or use bicycle helmets.

- Use overalls and footed sleepers as Space Suits. Pull large white socks over shoes for moon walkers or space shoes.

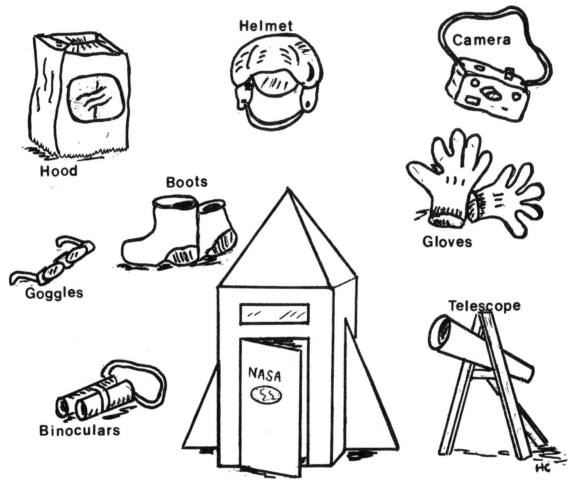

Helmet

Camera

Hood

Boots

Gloves

Goggles

Telescope

NASA

Binoculars

Alligator Bottles
Tear bits of masking tape and stick in overlapping pattern over entire surface of a bottle, jar or can. Rub shoe polish over the surface to create the "alligator" texture. The finished products serve as candle holders, pencil containers, vases, etc.

Yarn and String Bottles
Dip yarn and string in white glue and wind around bottles, cans and small boxes. Dry. Paint. Shellac after thoroughly dry.

Bottle Castings
Press designs into mud or wet sand using the bottom of a bottle. Fill forms with plaster of paris, add feathers, pebbles and other natural materials. Dry, remove castings, paint and decorate to create 3-D plaques.

Wire, Yarn and Thread Designs

Drive rows of small finish or box nails into small boards. Wind colored yarns, wire and threads into 3-D, geometric designs.

Easel Lifts

"Lift" designs from the dried layers and blobs of paint collected on the surface of easels. Lay wet paper towels or tissue paper against the paint and gently press the paper into the paint. Lift away carefully and hang to dry.

- Tape tissue paper to easel surface, paint with water to draw paint through.

- Use the papers to make tissue flowers and other projects.

Flowers

Bend one end of a pipe cleaner into petal shape, leaving enough "stem" to twist several petals together.

Dip petal into white glue and press on cloth or tissue scraps. Dry. Trim edges.

Bend several petals into a flower.

Make leaves in the same manner and twist to the stem.

Twist Together

Tie Dying (India, and Africa)

Dye designs in cloth by tying off or making knots in sections of fabric. Sheeting, cotton T–shirts, pillow cases). Dip tied sections and knots into dye.

Various methods are:

- Scrunch and Bunch sections of fabric. Wrap tightly with rubber bands and dip. You can also squeeze undiluted dye into the bunches before dipping into dye bath.

- Tie Knots in sections of fabric. Squeeze additional colors into knots before dipping.

- Rosette Knot. Pinch a section of fabric into "stem." Wrap *tightly* with elastic. A ring of stems creates a sunburst effect.

Flags and Banners

- Paint or tie dye designs to make group and individual flags.

- Print designs using paint with wood blocks and potato printers.

- Dot with juices from raw beets, strawberries and blueberries.

- Pound colors into cloth from leaves and flower petals.

People and Creatures

Cranberry and Twig Figures

Create people, animals and sculptures by connecting cranberries with twigs. The figures strengthen as the berries dry.

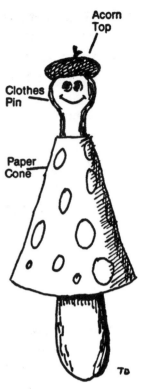

Acorn
Top

Clothes
Pin

Paper
Cone

| up ↑ 4 | **Clothespin People**
Cut a *small* "x" slit in a 3" (approx.) diameter circle of cloth or paper. Push over the head of the pin. Tie or tape at the "neck." Add acorn caps or paper cone hats to the clothespin. |

| up ↑ 4 | **Rock-Niks and Pebble People**
Glue rocks together to form creatures. Paint features with acrylics. Add feathers, ears, tails, caps, etc. |

Cloth Projects

| up ↑ 4 | **Grass Weaving**
• Weave grass, long leaves (day lilies), reeds, etc. into strips cut into panels of cloth.
• Make baskets by weaving cloth strips, grasses, yarns etc. into plastic and mesh vegetable bags and boxes. |

JUST FOR FUN

| up ↑ 3 | **Backwards Day**
Do everything backwards! Wear clothing backwards! Say "Goodbye!" at the beginning of the day. Start a meal with dessert. Read and *tell* stories from end to finish. Have backwards races, walk backwards. |

| up ↑ 4 | **Puppet Day**
• Provide a variety of materials and designs (samples) for puppet making—socks, paper bags, boxes, finger puppet items, paper tubes, plastic bottles and caps.
• Choose story (plot) ideas for using puppets to create a show.
• Plan and practice various acts and presentations. (Some children may just tell how their puppets were made and give the puppets names.)
• Present puppets. Play puppet games. Draw and photograph puppets. Sing and dance with puppets. |

| up ↑ 4 | **Carnival Day/Games of Chance**
• Decorate with streamers, flags, banners.
• Set up tents, tables, large carton booths, etc., each with a different game. Some suggestions: |

Pitch tennis balls into a large tin can set on the floor or fastened to a pole.

Roll ping-pong balls into a muffin tin set on a slant.

Drop clothespins into a wide-mouthed bottle.

Toss pennies or buttons onto numbered saucers floating in a tub of water.

Throw wet sponges at the face of a teacher (or a child who volunteers) poked through a hole in a sheet.

Pound a nail into a block of wood in fewest blows possible.

Toss jar rubbers or rings made by cutting the centers from plastic can lids onto a board with numbered cup hooks.

Hat and Bonnet Day
Provide circles, cones, bags, small boxes, old hats, etc.

Decorate with ribbons, feathers, bows, stickers, paper flowers, streamers, trims, etc.

Have a fashion show.

Story Book Day

- Children dress as characters in story books. (See October—CREATIVE PROJECTS— *T-Shirt and Paper Bag Costumes*)

- In the morning, children plan action and rehearse. Very young children can do this by "acting out" the story as the teacher reads it aloud.

- In the afternoon, children "put on" their story-plays for each other.

CHILDREN are like mirrors. They will reflect speech, diction, and mannerisms, and they will be secure if the teacher is calm and self-confident.

SEQUENCE TWELVE

AUGUST

AUGUST THEMES

AUGUST

Monkeys, Pinwheels & Space Tubes

Weather! Too hot, too cold, too dry or wet—is the weather ever just right? In New England, talking about the weather is practically a sport! But, no matter where we live, or what we consider "good" weather, everybody is affected—physically and emotionally—by weather. Some say, "Rain, rain, go away"; others sport bumper stickers saying "Think snow." Older folks say "I feel it in my bones." Young children can be unsettled and overstimulated by weather extremes—especially *wind*.

Weather forecasters, aviators, athletes, campers, hikers and other *vacationers* watch *clouds* and other weather conditions to plan work or play. August science activities offer ideas for amateur meteorologists.

As you plan outside activities, be prepared for instant changes as you dash inside from a downpour. Rain gear and a change of clothing are musts for enjoying *rainy days* outside. When special events—*Picnic Day, Pirate Day, Track Meets*, are rained out and "rained inside"—a positive (and adventurous) attitude and good preparation are crucial for a successful program.

Are there *toxic plants* in the area? Staff must investigate, point out dangers or post "Do Not Touch" warnings. *Poison Hotline* numbers and emergency procedures must be reviewed.

Vacationers pack suitcases. Children can practice *packing skills* and help parents to organize and pack suitcases or camping gear ("Did you pack your teddy bear?") *Travel games* are suggested for restless riders.

Two triangles, when put together, make a (baseball) *diamond*. Beanbags in all kinds of shapes can be tossed onto matching *shapes*.

Science activities include *wind* and *flight experiments* with *paper airplanes, parachutes* and *pinwheels; vibration experiments* with *"space tubes," "ripplers," bells* and *chimes. Monkeys* are familiar African animals, but have you heard of a <u>hyraxe</u> or a <u>duilar</u>? Perhaps you will become a local expert on African <u>aoudads</u>.

It's August! Backyard gardeners lament "I can't possibly use all these *tomatoes*. Would you like some?" How many ways can the children use tomatoes at a Tomato Festival? Tired of eating tomatoes? Make *tabulleh* and *hummus* and serve in *pita pockets* on *picnic day*.

Tomatoes are red. Sky is *blue*. How many shades of blue can we find and name?

Everyone is a super athlete at the track meet (and a good sport)—JUST FOR FUN!

SEQUENCE TWELVE

PEOPLE

up ↑ 4

Weather Forecasters/Meteorologist
What do children understand about this work? Do forecasters make or control the weather? Why is this work important? Does work or play sometimes get cancelled due to weather?

Invite a local TV or radio weather forecaster to come and describe the job and suggest ways children can participate in weather watching activities.

up ↑ 4

Aviation Workers
- What and who travel on airplanes? (Products, mail, food; vacation and business fliers; medical emergency doctors; weather forecasting and research; military fliers; crop dusting; fire fighters.)
- Collect pictures that show different uses of planes and helicopters.
- What do the pilot and co-pilot do? Who else works on a large passenger plane? Who are the aviation workers who are not on the plane and what are their jobs? (Mechanics, flight schedulers, weather operators, air traffic controllers, ground crew, etc.)
- Collect pictures of people connected with aviation. Make a mural or collage with both sets of pictures.

up ↑ 4

Sports and Athletes
Show pictures of sports and equipment—balls, bats, gloves, rackets, knee guards, golf clubs, hiking gear, skates, etc. What sports are familiar to the children? Who are their heros and heroines? What sports do parents play?

- Make a display of different sizes and kinds of balls used in sports. Arrange by size. Identify the sport.
- Set up a golf course. Putt balls into holes, tunnels, chutes and boxes, with brooms or croquet mallets.
- Toss balls and balloons over nets.
- Hold races with toy cars on ramps and chutes.
- Play simplified ball games—tag ball, kick ball, basketball.

SCHOOL AGE

- What is the difference between amateur and professional athletes? Name well-known teams from each category. (College teams—amateur. NBA, NFL, etc. teams—professional.) Which are their favorite teams?
- What are the Olympics? What kinds of events are included?
- What is a triathlon?
- What special abilities and characteristics does a professional baseball player, football player, ice skater, etc. need?

(See also JUST FOR FUN—*Track Meet*)

EXPANDING OUR WORLD

Weather Station

Visit a broadcasting station to see computers, weather maps and forecasters at work. Some tall buildings have weather instruments on roof tops.

Houseboat, Tent, Trailer/Vacations

* Take children inside a houseboat, tent or trailer. How are they different from houses or apartments?

* Plan a compact living space. How much furniture and equipment do you need? What can you go without? Pack a suitcase with only items needed for a week's vacation.

* Set up a campsite using pup tents (blankets). Children share a day's activities, snacks, nap times in pairs. Group comes together to discuss experiences and problems.

SKILLS FOR DAILY LIVING

Packing

* Ask children if they ever go away with their parents for a week-end? To visit grandparents? Cousins? Stay in a motel? What kinds of things do they need to take?

* Bring in an assortment of children's clothing for different seasons. (Warm and light pajamas; bathing suit and winter jacket; play clothes and party clothes; shorts and ski pants; mittens and scarves.) Lay them out and ask what they would pack in August? In January?

* Ask what else they would need (hairbrush, toothbrush, socks, underwear).

* Provide a small suitcase to pack. Does everything fit? Do they have to leave something, or can they repack it so things *will* fit?

* Help children make a checklist to use when they pack for themselves.

Poisonous Plants

* Show pictures (or point to real plants) of poison ivy and poison oak. Say: "Stay away from these plants. They can cause a red rash that itches terribly and sometimes makes people *very* sick."

* Check information about indoor house plants. Some common species are poisonous.

* Show pictures or samples of such plants as oleander, nightshade, yew, foxglove and privet. Say: "*Never* eat the berries or leaves of a plant unless an adult has given them to you."

Note to teachers: Look in the front of your telephone book to find a POISON Hotline. Investigate areas in which the children play to identify plants and berries. If you are in doubt about their toxicity, call the Hotline and ask. When a child eats *anything* you suspect is toxic, call for help at once! Take a sample of the plant or other material with you if medical help is necessary.

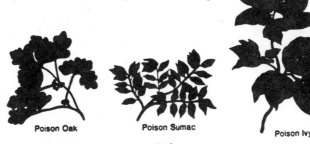

Poison Oak   Poison Sumac   Poison Ivy

CONCEPTS

up ↑ 3 *Tube Game (In/Out, Back/Forth, Left/Right)*

Tape paper tissue and towel tubes inside a shallow box. Leave space around open ends and between tubes for a small ball (ping-pong size) to roll freely.

- Tip the box to move the rolling ball in and out of the tubes.

- Mark the course which the ball must follow with arrows.

- Variation: Tape tubes in the same direction, side-by-side, leaving spaces at top and bottom for the rolling ball. Number the tubes. Player tries to roll the ball down one tube, up the next, etc. to complete the course.

- Player tries to roll through highest number—or calls a number and tries to roll through the tube numbered to match.

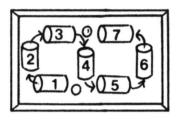 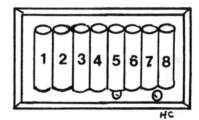

5 ↑ 3 *Blue*

- Children collect samples of different shades of blue. Paste blue shades of paper onto a mural design.

- Look for blue in nature—sky, flowers, water, insects and berries.

- Collect and make a poster of words that name a shade of blue.

- Ask: "How many children are wearing something blue?"

up ↑ 3 *Bean Bag Shape Toss*

- Make round, square and triangular bean bags. Use a different fabric for each shape. Cut shapes from fabrics to match the bags. Glue shapes to cardboard panels. Children try to toss bags onto their matching shapes.

- Cut shape holes in the side of a carton. Toss the matching shapes through the holes.

SCIENCE

up ↑ 4 *Tomatoes*

Ask children to list foods containing and made with tomatoes (soup, sauce, catsup, relish, salsa, etc.)

Peel a tomato. Slice a tomato. Squeeze out the juice.

Taste green and red tomatoes, small (cherry), medium (plum), and large (beef steak) varieties.

Serve fresh and cooked tomatoes in recipes which the children prepare.

up ↑ 4 *Chick Peas/Hummus (Multi-cultural, Middle East)*

Serve whole in soup and salad. Compare tastes of chick peas, kidney beans, lentils and other legumes.

Make a chick pea spread or dip called hummus. Grind or mash chick peas and season with lemon, salt, garlic, various herbs. Serve in pita pockets, on toast, crackers, etc.

Tabulleh (Multi-cultural, Middle East) (Recipe)

1 cup extra fine bulgar	juice of small lemon
large bunch of parsley	1/2 tsp salt
small onion, finely chopped	1/4 cup vegetable oil
8-10 mint leaves *or* 1 tsp dried mint	1 medium tomato, chopped

Directions:

Soak bulgar for about 30 minutes, or until all the water has been absorbed. Mark container at level of dry, then soaked bulgar. Ask: "Where has the water gone?"

Wash and chop parsley, or cut into fine bits (with children's scissors).

Chop onion, cut mint, squeeze lemon, chop tomato.

Squeeze bulgar in a cloth to remove excess water. Mix with other ingredients. Chill for 30 minutes.

Serve in pita pockets or bowls. Add yogurt as desired.

Monkey, Ape, Gorilla, Chimpanzee

What do the children know about "monkeys"? Are they all the same? Where do they live? What do they eat? Explore this popular animal in all the ways you can.

- Have a Monkey Day with songs, motions, stories, tricks ("monkey shines" and "monkey business").
- Serve bananas whole, in slices, on ice cream, in milk shakes.

Corn

- Uproot a fully grown plant (or visit a farm), harvest the ears, remove husks and cook. Taste corn oil.
- Use the silk and husks in projects such as making dolls.
- Walk through the rows at a farm to experience the size of growing corn.

(See also October Sequence for Corn Activities)

Wind Work

How does wind work for us? (Wind mills, weather vane, kite, pin wheel, sail boat, air craft, clothes line.) What machines use man-made "wind" (air)? (Hair and clothes driers, vacuum cleaner, musical instruments.)

Wash dolls' clothes and blankets on a windy day. Hang some inside and some outside. Notice which dries more quickly.

Wind Indicators

How do we know the wind is blowing? Use senses to observe: trees and shrubs moving; pressure against the body; leaves rustling; smells of smoke; salt spray; blossoms; exhaust; clothes blowing on a line; windsock.

- Look for weather vanes. What direction is the wind blowing? Why is it important to know this? Wet a finger and feel the wind direction.
- Read *Hi Mister Robin* by Alvin Tresselt (pub. Lothrop) and *Gilberto and the Wind* by Marie Hall Ets (pub. Viking).

Wind Sock Weather Vane

up ↑ 5

Construct a simple weather vane outside to show wind direction. Attach a nylon cloth tube to a dowel with crossed sticks on top indicating directions. Use a compass to set direction pointers.

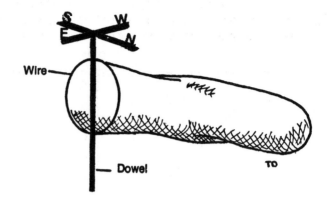

Sock should turn freely around the dowel as the wind blows.

Listen to weather reports on windy days. Check to see if the prevailing winds predicted are the same as those shown by your wind sock.

Wind Storms

up ↑ 5

What are tornados? Hurricanes? Typhoons? Have any children experienced them? Ask them to describe the experience.

Each day, ask the children to describe the weather. Based on these ideas, give *each* day a name, as the Weather Bureau names wind storms. Use the children's names in alphabetical order in the daily weather names: Breezy Betty, Foggy Fred, Huffy Helen, Jittery Jerry, Sizzling Sam, etc.

Dust Bowl/Erosion

up ↑ 5

"Plant" gardens by laying pictures of plants or paper circles on paper squares. Lay out the gardens in rows on the floor.

Turn on a fan. What happens? Describe the "Dust Bowl" and other such wind erosion effects. Are there any such erosion areas nearby to see?

- Dust Bowl Game. Each child or team uses marked garden plots and plants. After the wind storm, each child or team retrieves and replants the gardens. Play Dust Bowl as a relay race with older children.

SCHOOL AGE

- Outside. Line off squares and sprinkle sand or dry soil. Blow away with a fan. Rebuild gardens using wet soil. Blow with fan once again.

Helicopter Twirls

up ↑ 4

- Cut the shape shown in illustration from sturdy paper. Cut along solid lines. Bend on dotted lines as shown. Attach paper clip to "tail" to weight. Drop from heights and spin.

- Collect winged maple seeds. Drop from high places. How are they different from seeds without wings? Why do seeds need wings?

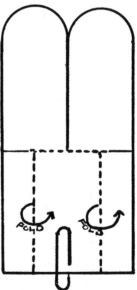

Cut on Solid Line
Fold on Dotted Line

Parachutes

up ↑ 3

Tie strings (6" to 8") to the corners of a square of sheer fabric or tissue paper. Attach string ends to small corks or toy people.

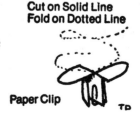

Paper Clip

up
↑
5

Pinwheel

Cut a 5" square of sturdy paper. Cut slits from points to 1" from the center hole. Punch holes at each corner. Bring points to the center and fasten with a straight pin or small brad to a stick. Allow slack on the pin so wheel can spin.

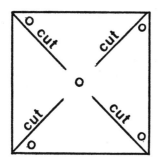 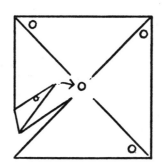 

up
↑
4

Airplane

Fold a rectangle of paper, the long way, in the center and open out (1). Fold points (A) to the center fold. Fold new points (B) to the center (2). Refold along center line with the folded edges on the outside. Fold upper edges to lower fold, forming wings.

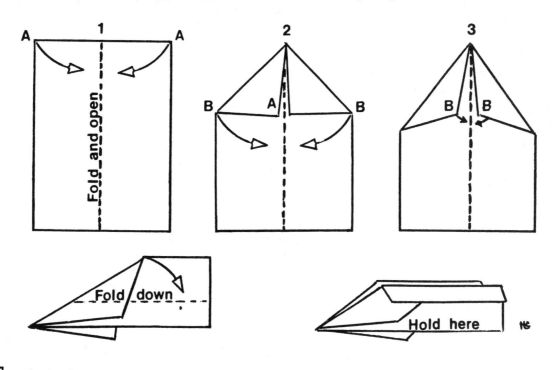

up
↑
4

Bird Plane

Fold a sturdy paper rectangle in half the long way. Draw a bird outline as shown. Cut out the shape, keeping the fold at the bottom. Paste body and head together at the fold, keeping the wings free. Dry. Fold wing tips down and fly.

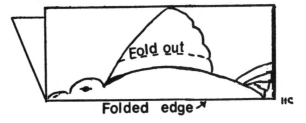

up ↑ 5 *Clouds*

- To demonstrate how moist air rises and forms clouds, place a dish of hot water in a cool room or outside. The steam rising is a "cloud," formed when cold air and moist air combine.

- Clouds heavy with moisture form raindrops. Place a sponge (cloud) in a cloth "sling" or colander. Saturate sponge with water until the sponge drips (rain).

- Hold a pan of ice cubes over a boiling kettle. Drops (cloud) form on the bottom of the pan (condensation). As the rising steam forms larger drops they fall (rain).

up ↑ 5 *Humidity*

Use two household (liquid) thermometers. Wrap a strip of cotton cloth around the bulb of one thermometer, leaving a long end of the strip free. Hang this strip in a can of water to act as a wick. Keep the can filled. (See July—SCIENCE—*Capillary Action*)

Place this "wet bulb" thermometer beside the second "dry bulb."

As water evaporates the "wet bulb" will give a lower reading. Dry days cause a greater difference between the two thermometers. When the two readings are the same, the humidity is 100%.

up ↑ 3 *Absorption of Heat*

Place a coin on an ice cube. The coin will melt an impression into the ice cube. The coin is warmer; the ice absorbs the heat.

MUSIC—MOVEMENT

5 ↑ 3 *—Ing Words*

- Talk about words ending with —ing. (Running, jumping, laughing, touching, talking, chewing, etc.)

- Ask each child to choose and demonstrate the motions. Others guess the word.

- Do the —ing motions slowly, quickly, high and low, left and right, etc.

- Make —ing motions in a tiny space, a big space, backwards (as appropriate), etc.

- What are morning —ing words (shaving, washing, cooking)? Baby's —ing words (nursing, cooing, wetting, fussing)?

- What are travel —ing words (packing, driving, flying, waving)?

up ↑ 5 *Rhythm Pattern Pictures*

Children work on the floor or at easels with wax crayons and large paper. Play musical selections with various rhythms, tempos, moods and dynamics.

- Begin by some practice *suggestions*, making motions in the air—dots and dashes (choppy rhythms); wavy, sweeping lines (long, melodic phrases); long lines (long beats); dark colors (low, solemn music); light colors (high notes). Talk about moods, bold colors, rhythms, etc.

- Children use crayons to draw designs as *they* feel about the music.

"Telephone" in the Wilderness (Auditory Game, Multi-cultural)

Divide into tribal groups. Choose names suggested by African, South American, Native American, etc. cultures.

- Communicate from different rooms, outside areas or on two sides of a curtain, using rhythm patterns and other sounds. One group makes a sound and a rhythmic pattern. Other group repeats. Begin with two groups. Gradually move groups apart and break into smaller units. End session with a large ring of children passing the sound and rhythm along until the first child receives it back.

- Play hide and seek in small groups using the sounds and rhythms.

- Use various natural objects to create sounds (sticks, stones, tree trunks, leafy branches, water, shell chimes, etc.)

(See July—LANGUAGE—DRAMA—*African Names*)

 ### *Music Day*

Invite instrumentalists to play and demonstrate their music.

Set up laboratories and sound booths featuring individual families of instruments. Feature tapes and recordings playing music of each group. Decorate areas with pictures of instruments and musicians.

- Percussion booth—Drums, sticks, shakers, rattles, xylophones, triangles.

- Bells—arrange from the tiniest to largest.

- String instruments—guitar, auto harp, banjo.

- Flutes and whistles—kazoo, harmonica.

- Provide materials to make various instruments at each booth. Children decide which laboratory to visit. Groups join at a Grand Jamboree at the end of the day to play and demonstrate each instrument family.

Homemade Instruments

Teach children to respect and care for homemade musical instruments as you would protect a rare Stradivarius violin. Whether a coffee can drum, two dowel rhythm sticks or pie plate tambourine, each instrument has a name, a special storage box or shelf and is used with care. Instruments are returned after each use.

 ### *Bells and Chimes*

- Tie large nails and spikes of graduated sizes from a dowel or coat hanger. Space 1" apart. Use approximately 6" lengths of string. Use a table knife or metal rod as a striker.

- Shell chime—string shells with naturally occurring holes and hang along a dowel or hanger or in clusters from a stick.

- Plant pot chime—choose eight clay plant pots. Suspend on a rope knotted through the drain hole and test to approximate eight scale tones. Hang eight scale-tuned pots from a *sturdy* wooden frame.

 Plastic Pen

 Pastry Brush

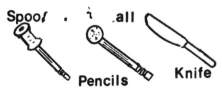 **Spool** **.all** **Pencils** **Knife**

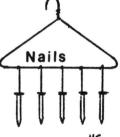 **Nails**

HC

Space Tube Vibrator

<table><tr><td>up</td></tr><tr><td>↑</td></tr><tr><td>4</td></tr></table>

• Stretch a "slinky" spring through a long cardboard or plastic (4 inch) tube. Attach both spring ends to the tube. Strike and shake the tube to create "eerie" sounds.

• Use various other springs through smaller tubes in the same manner.

Sand Blocks

<table><tr><td>up</td></tr><tr><td>↑</td></tr><tr><td>4</td></tr></table>

Nail or glue sandpaper to woodblocks and attach knob handles.

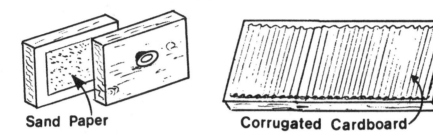

Sand Paper   Corrugated Cardboard

Wash Board "Rippler"

<table><tr><td>up</td></tr><tr><td>↑</td></tr><tr><td>4</td></tr></table>

Glue or nail, with flat head, short roofing nails, pieces of corrugated cardboard packing materials to a board and rub across the surface with strikers.

Rain/Storm Sounds

<table><tr><td>up</td></tr><tr><td>↑</td></tr><tr><td>3</td></tr></table>

Walk in the rain. Carry umbrellas. Stand under trees, plastic and canvas shelters, metal roofs, under drip edge and gutters. Walk on sand, pavement, by water in ponds, puddles and on grass. Walk in woods, fields and on bridges.

Stand inside screened porches, under wood decks, by open windows. Sit in cars and vans.

• After the rain walk, use various instruments and sounds by voice and objects to recreate the sounds of rain. Develop and name the sounds—drip, splash, whoosh, trickle, gush, pitter-patter, etc.

• Recreate a rainstorm cycle from the slow gentle drizzle, to a downpour with wind, back down to the last dripping of drops onto different surfaces.

   Leader "orchestrates" the sounds, directing groups using different instruments, alone and in clusters, making the sound effects. Storm builds up as instruments are added and gradually dies down as they fade away.

• Repeat the experience by taking an imaginary walk.

Squooshers

<table><tr><td>5</td></tr><tr><td>↑</td></tr><tr><td>3</td></tr></table>

• Nail oversized sneakers, crêpe-sole shoes, deck shoes, rubbers, etc. to a board in walking positions, so children can easily step from one to another. Fill shoes with water. Step in, tread to make squooshing noises.

• Nail shoes side by side. Wet to make a squooshy treader, or pull on several pairs of heavy socks and tread in pans of shallow water.

LANGUAGE—DRAMA

⁵↑₃ *Monkey Business (Story Development)*

Read *Caps for Sale* by E. Slobodkina (pub. Scholastic). Develop activities, some suggested below, based on this story and others. DO NOT TRY ALL THE SUGGESTED ACTIVITIES AT ONE TIME.

- Peddlers. What do they do?
- Make paper hats. "Gather" materials and make imaginary caps. Describe them. (See CREATIVE PROJECTS—*Paper Hats*)
- Take turns peddling the hats. Walk with several hats stacked on heads.
- Be monkeys, cavorting, saying "chee, chee," wiggling, hopping, falling from trees.
- Discuss the tricks played on each other by peddler and monkeys.
- Make a mural or felt board using monkeys, tree, caps, peddler, etc.
- Develop counting and color sorting games using caps and monkeys' vests.
- Re-enact the story, being monkeys, peddler, etc. Use rhythm patterns and instruments to create sound effects, i.e. sand block for "chee, chee."
- Develop concepts—on top; back to (tree); threw down; looked up; left and right.
- Mime the story actions—no words.

up↑₄ *Monkey Tree (Various Concepts)*

- Cut monkey shapes from cardboard. Glue on fuzzy, brown fabric. Attach pipe cleaner tails. Add paper vests and hats in various colors, attached to monkeys with "velcro" or yarn loops. Hang monkeys on a twiggy branch set in a cement base (can) or from a cardboard tree with paper pockets. Add numerals and letters to monkeys and garments.
- Play matching and guessing games; re-enact the story; arrange monkeys by letters and numbers; match colors of caps and vests; hang monkeys "high," "low," "beside,".
- Make play money and sell caps and vests.

up↑₄ *Airport and Travel Day*

Transform the room into an airport—runways with boards or chalk lines; a control tower; props such as telephones, flashlights, signal flags, ticket counters, travel fliers, maps. Activities might be "programmed" to last throughout a day, perhaps based on taking a trans-oceanic flight. Children choose destination, plan and pack, purchase tickets, fly and return.

- Make suitcases (cartons with rope handles); baggage checks.
- Flight attendants seat passengers, hand out pillows and snacks.
- Passengers sit in rows, eat snacks from trays, watch in-flight movies.
- Families and friends welcome traveler home at day's end.

Imaginary Picnic

Each child has a basket (or small box with string handles) and a cloth napkin.

- Paper plates or trays are passed around, each with imaginary foods. "Would you like tuna fish or cheese sandwiches? Red or green grapes?" "These are carrot and celery sticks. How many will you take?" Children choose imaginary foods—"I choose tuna fish, an apple and some milk."

- Go for walk, choose a picnic site (inside or outside). Spread a picnic blanket. Children sit in a circle, spread their napkins and take turns telling what their lunches contain. (Did any ants come?)

CREATIVE PROJECTS

Travel Games

- Line a shallow box with green paper (grass), paste in black strips (roads). Add tubes for tunnels, small boxes with cardboard ramps (bridges), small boxes for garages and houses. Furnish small vehicles and people to fit the roadway. (Ask parents to supply boxes.)

- Find two sets of identical pictures of things seen along the highway. Paste one set into books with pockets stapled along the bottom edge. (Used envelopes)

  Paste the matching pictures on cards to fit the pockets.

  Variation: Ask parents to supply travel/vacation brochures showing places they plan to visit. Children can make matching games to take along on trips.

Weaving

Wind twine (warps) around sturdy, shallow cardboard boxes, empty picture frames, small board sections.

Tear cloth into strips and weave into warp. Cut warp loops, stitch ends to prevent raveling.

Braiding

- Attach three strands of cloth strips to trees, fences, or hooks, and braid.

- Tie long 10' to 12' cloth strips or ropes. Three children each hold a strand and take turns crossing each other's strands as they walk in braiding motions.

- Use braids to wind and weave small mats; on puppets and portraits; as handles and tie belts.

Giants

- Collect boxes, cartons, tubes, cans, bottle tops, wire, and elegant junk. Assemble giant creatures. Paint, decorate and name creatures.

- Discuss "scary" and "horrible" creatures. Talk about fears to help allay misconceptions about ogres and monsters. Make up stories.

JUST FOR FUN

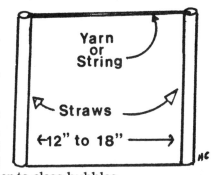

up ↑ 4 | *Window Pane Bubbles*

- Use recipe from September—JUST FOR FUN— *Bubbles.*

- Make "frames" with plastic straws and string or yarn.

- Hold frame by the straws. Dip into bubble solution to soak yarn or string. Pull taut, gently lift frame, forming a bubble pane between the strings. Lift slowly and smoothly, also sideways to form long irregular bubbles. *Practice* bringing straws together to close bubbles.

up ↑ 4 | *Table Bubbles*

Pour a saucer-sized circle of bubble solution on a smooth tabletop (metal, formica) or tray. Spread solution to about 12" circle. Hold a plastic straw into solution, not quite touching the table. Gently blow bubbles. Put straw *through* a bubble and blow another inside and beside. Make clusters of bubbles.

up ↑ 4 | *Paper Cup Sculptures*

- Save used paper cups. Use straws, paper punch, string, paper clips, tape, to build sculptures, model cities, creatures, collages, space stations, etc.

- Hold a modeler's "convention" where each child (or group) tells about the creations.

up ↑ 5 | *Paper Hat*

Fold a newspaper sheet in half. Fold top corners down to meet at the center. Fold bottom edges up at front and back (hat sides) to form a cuff. Fasten ends of cuffs with a staple to hold in place.

- Variation: Fold back one point (D) to form a fireman's hat.

- Paint newspaper pages and dry to make colored hats.

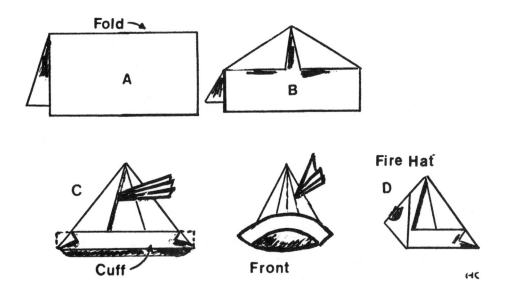

August

Pirate Day

up ↑ 3

- Make costumes using eye patches, kerchiefs, tunics, paper swords, beards, etc. Wrap round crackers in foil for "pieces of eight" treasure. Make a treasure map, using playground or building items as markers.
- One group hides, another searches for treasure using the map.
- Make carton boats with seat block seats. "Fire" ping-pong balls and crumpled papers into opposing boats.
- Lay out stepping stones to follow to an island.
- Fish, with magnets, from a blue lagoon (wading pool).
- Walk a plank and jump into the lagoon.
- Tell "Peter Pan" stories, play the music.

Picnic Day

up ↑ 2

- Prepare picnic lunches for several different groups. Each has a picnic at a different place around the center, neighborhood park, staff homes.
- Eat real picnics but at imaginary "beaches," "mountaintops," "beside streams."
- Groups come together to tell about various adventures.

Track Meet

up ↑ 3

Plan as a surprise, especially inside during rainy weather. Some suggestions:

Shot-put with balloons or blown up paper bags.

High jump from standing position with broomstick.

Broad jump from standing position.

Javelin throw with drinking straws.

Discus throw with paper plates.

Standing broad grin—measure width of grins.

Running high whistle—time length of sustained whistle.

Feather blow relay—blow a feather 25 ft. using relay teams.

Foot race—measure combined length of both feet.

Stacking straws two by two, in alternating directions. Older children stack on top of a wide-mouthed jar.

Stacking toothpicks on a small mouth bottle.

INDEX—PART ONE

ACTIVITIES LISTED UNDER MAIN HEADINGS

INDEX—PART TWO

ALPHABETICAL LISTING OF ALL ACTIVITIES

MUST READING

FOR EARLY CHILDHOOD EDUCATORS

I Am! I Can! (New and Revised)

　　Volume One　　*Keys to Quality Child Care*

　　　　　　　　　A Guide for Directors

　　　　　　　　　　　　by Grace L. Mitchell, Nancy C. Bailey, Lois F. Dewsnap

　　Volume Two　　*A Preschool Curriculum*

　　　　　　　　　Activities for the Classroom

　　　　　　　　　　　　by Harriet Chmela, Grace L. Mitchell, Lois F. Dewsnap

A Very Practical Guide to Discipline with Young Children　　　　by Grace L. Mitchell, Ph.D.

The Day Care Book　　　　　　　　　　　　by Grace L. Mitchell, Ph.D.

Curriculum Planner for Early Childhood Teachers

　　　　　　　　　　　　by Nancy C. Bailey and Marcia Bennett-Hebert

Ages and Stages　　　　　　　　　　　　by Karen Miller

Things To Do with Toddlers and Twos　　　　　　　　by Karen Miller

MORE Things To Do with Toddlers and Twos　　　　　　by Karen Miller

---

Also available:

Early Childhood Staff Training Center　　　by Grace L. Mitchell, Ph.D. and Lois Dewsnap, M.A.

　　A ten-session videotaped staff training program with an Instructor's Guide, a Test Packet, and five related books.

For information about the training program, write to:

　　TelShare Publishing Company, Inc.
　　24 Breakwater Drive
　　Chelsea, MA 02150

Or call:　　**1 (800) 343-9707** (outside Massachusetts)

　　　　　　(617) 884-4404 (inside Massachusetts)